Creating Health Behavior Change

Developmental Clinical Psychology and Psychiatry Series

Series Editor: Alan E. Kazdin, Yale University

Recent volumes in this series . . .

Creating Health Behavior Change

How to Develop Community-Wide Programs for Youth

Cheryl L. Perry

*To Dan and Darcia
my best to you!
Cheryl*

Volume 43
Developmental Clinical Psychology and Psychiatry

SAGE Publications, Inc.
International Educational and Professional Publisher
Thousand Oaks   London   New Delhi

For information:

SAGE Publications, Inc.
2455 Teller Road
Thousand Oaks, California 91320
E-mail: order@sagepub.com

SAGE Publications Ltd.
6 Bonhill Street
London EC2A 4PU
United Kingdom

SAGE Publications India Pvt. Ltd.
M-32 Market
Greater Kailash I
New Delhi 110 048 India

Printed in the United States of America

Library of Congress Cataloging-in-Publication Data

Perry, Cheryl.
    Creating health behavior change: How to develop community-wide programs
for youth / by Cheryl L. Perry.
        p.   cm.—(Developmental clinical psychology and psychiatry series; v. 43)
    Includes bibliographical references and index.
    ISBN 0-7619-1226-6 (cloth: acid-free paper)
    ISBN 0-7619-1227-4 (pbk.: acid-free paper)
        1. Community health services for children.   2. Health promotion.   3. Health
education.   4. Health behavior in adolescence.   5. Child health services.
6. Health behavior in children.   I. Title.   II. Series: Developmental clinical
psychology and psychiatry; v. 43.
    RJ101 .P446   1999
    362.2'2'0835—dc21   99-6239

This book is printed on acid-free paper.

99   00   01   02   03   10   9   8   7   6   5   4   3   2   1

Acquiring Editor:	Kassie Gavrilis
Editorial Assistant:	Heidi Van Middlesworth
Production Editor:	Wendy Westgate
Production Assistant:	Patricia Zeman
Designer/Typesetter:	Janelle LeMaster
Indexer:	Molly Hall

CONTENTS

SERIES EDITOR'S INTRODUCTION

Interest in child development and adjustment is by no means new. Yet only recently has the study of children benefited from advances in both clinical and scientific research. Advances in the social and biological sciences, the emergence of disciplines and subdisciplines that focus exclusively on childhood and adolescence, and greater appreciation of the impact of such influences as the family, peers, and school have helped accelerate research on developmental psychopathology. Apart from interest in the study of child development and adjustment for its own sake, the need to address clinical problems of adulthood naturally draws one to investigate precursors in childhood and adolescence.

Within a relatively brief period, the study of psychopathology among children and adolescents has proliferated considerably. Several different professional journals, annual book series, and handbooks devoted entirely to the study of children and adolescents and their adjustment document the proliferation of work in the field. Nevertheless, there is a paucity of resource material that presents information in an authoritative, systematic, and disseminable fashion. There is a need within the field to convey the latest developments and to represent different disciplines, approaches, and conceptual views to the topics of childhood and adolescent adjustment and maladjustment.

The Sage Series on **Developmental Clinical Psychology and Psychiatry** is designed to uniquely serve several needs of the field. The Series encompasses individual monographs prepared by experts in the fields of clinical child psychology, child psychiatry, child development, and related disciplines. The primary focus is on developmental psychopathology, which refers broadly here to the diagnosis, assessment, treatment, and prevention of problems that arise in the period from infancy through adolescence. A working assumption of the Series is that understanding, identifying, and treating problems of youth must draw on multiple disciplines and diverse views within a given discipline.

The task for individual contributors is to present the latest theory and research on various topics, including specific types of dysfunction, diagnostic and treatment approaches, and special problem areas that affect adjustment. Core topics within clinical work are addressed by the Series. Authors are asked to bridge potential theory, research, and clinical practice and to outline the current status and future directions. The goals of the Series and the tasks presented to individual contributors are demanding. We have been extremely fortunate in recruiting leaders in the field who have been able to translate their recognized scholarship and expertise into highly readable works on contemporary topics.

The present book, by Dr. Cheryl Perry, examines community-wide interventions for children and adolescents. Such interventions have focused on reduction and prevention of cigarette smoking and alcohol and drug use and promotion of healthy eating, exercise, and safe sex, to mention some examples. Although the book reviews successful programs in these areas, the focus is much broader. The unique feature of the book is elaboration of the process of developing community-wide programs to promote health, broadly conceived as physical, psychological, social, and spiritual functioning. The book explains the steps in moving from theory and research to practice and describes the processes of developing, implementing, maintaining, and evaluating intervention programs. Concrete details, guidelines, and steps are provided and well illustrated for such processes as creating the intervention model, determining what type of program is most likely to be applicable and effective, and developing the specific intervention program. The recommendations reflect the remarkable experience the author has had in implementing and evaluating large-scale programs. The book can easily serve as a handbook for developing intervention programs in the community. Although the focus is on child and adolescent health, the model has applicability across the developmental spectrum in conveying how to move from research to application in promoting health.

ALAN E. KAZDIN, PhD

ACKNOWLEDGMENTS

There are many people to acknowledge and to thank for their help in the writing of this book. Because community-wide programs involve numerous people, including students, teachers, parents, school staff, community leaders, colleagues, and more, I'd first like to thank these people for their collaboration and trust over the past 22 years. Without their willingness to participate in health behavior research and to share their ideas and insights, the successes of our projects with young people would never have been realized.

I would also like to give heartfelt thanks to my very talented colleagues Bonnie Dudovitz, Leslie Lytle, Kelli Komro, DeAnn Lazovich, Bonnie Manning, Dianne Neumark-Sztainer, Mary Smyth, Melissa Stigler, Kathy Stolle-McAlister, Mary Story, Sara Veblen-Mortenson, and Carolyn Williams for their incisive and helpful comments on and assistance with this book.

Last, I'd like to thank my family, including my brother, Bob Perry, who is an exceptionally creative and dedicated teacher and whose work inspired me from an early age; my late parents, Robert and Marguerite Perry, for their unfailing personal support throughout their lives; and my husband, Sushil Kriplani, whose dedication to peacefulness and nourishment made the process of writing at home a joy.

The research reported in this book was funded by grants from the National Institutes of Health, the World Health Organization, and the John B. Hawley family. The Bush Faculty Sabbatical Award provided additional support for the writing of the book.

1

INTRODUCTION

We might all agree that it "takes a community to raise a child," but there is very little agreement on how to accomplish this. Some argue that it mostly takes conscientious parents to raise a child; others argue that good schools are responsible for preparing the young for society; still others will point to the complexity of our culture and the information age, with advertising, television, videos, the Internet, and music that now teach our young how to behave. Indeed, children are influenced by and learn from all of these realms of society. How, then, can we influence them positively? How do we create communities that support the healthy development of children and adolescents? A community-wide approach uses the resources of all the systems of a child's social environment, enhances each system to optimize development, and, particularly important, attempts to coordinate efforts across systems.

The purpose of this book is to provide a process for the development of effective community-wide health behavior programs for children and adolescents. The process can be applied to health behavior programs among adults, but this book focuses on youth. Before beginning to describe this process, it may be useful to explain why a "process" is important, define some terms, and provide the research context that has generated this process and the need for such a book.

A process for developing community-wide health behavior programs is clearly needed. The goal of these programs is to make changes in identified health behaviors. Yet relatively few published programs with adequate evaluations have been successful in changing the health behavior of youth. For example, a recently published book titled *Making the Grade: A Guide to School Drug Prevention Programs* examined 47 school-based tobacco, alcohol, and drug use prevention programs that have been nationally disseminated in the United States and found that only 10 of those programs had published evaluations in peer-reviewed journals with acceptable methodology, and only 6 of the programs were rated as excellent (Drug Strategies, 1996). Even successful programs have tended to lose their potency when disseminated more widely. Replications of two successful smoking prevention programs in Minnesota (Murray et al., 1992) and in Texas (Parcel, Eriksen, Lovato, Gottlieb, & Brink, 1989) found very little impact on adolescent smoking rates when more widely disseminated. In part, this may be the result of not adhering to those aspects of the program that are most potent and responsible for behavior change. Because wider dissemination depends on the decisions of people at the community level—school staff, parents, community officials—recognition of what is needed to create a program with the potential to "work," that is, for a program to result in behavior change, needs to be more broadly disseminated as well. For example, a potent component of smoking and alcohol use prevention programs is the use of trained peer leaders to conduct the programs (Arkin, Roemhild, Johnson, Luepker, & Murray, 1981; Black, Tobler, & Sciacca, 1998; Klepp, Halper, & Perry, 1986; Perry, Grant, et al. 1989; Perry et al., 1996). However, selecting and training peer leaders is an unusual procedure in schools, and it requires commitment of time and personnel. Those involved in implementing the programs may not be aware of the important contribution of peer leaders to the behavioral strength of a prevention program. For these and other reasons, the peer leader component has often been modified or eliminated when the programs are disseminated. Thus, a broader understanding of the process of developing a successful health behavior program should lead to the implementation of more effective programs.

Significant behavior change among children and adolescents across a variety of behaviors and community-based research studies has been achieved through health behavior programs based on the process presented in this book. For example, smoking prevention programs that have targeted the social-environmental influences to smoke, rather than knowledge of the harmful consequences of smoking, have repeatedly delayed the onset of smoking among young adolescents (U.S. Department of Health and Human Services [USDHHS], 1994). Programs that have emphasized new role models of healthy eating, skills to select and prepare foods, and reinforcement for participation have resulted in healthier eating patterns among youth (Contento et al., 1995; Luepker et al., 1996; Perry et al., 1998; Perry, Mullis, & Maile, 1985). Programs that have had multiple components—so that changes occurred in classrooms, with parents, in the school environment, and in the whole community—have resulted in greater changes in healthy behavior among young people than programs that were restricted to the classroom alone (Luepker et al., 1996; Perry, 1998; Perry, Bishop, et al., 1998; Perry et al., 1988; Perry, Williams, et al., 1996). Thus, the application of the process of creating health behavior programs that is presented in this book has already been shown to be efficacious in multiple research studies. The challenge is to apply this process more broadly, outside the research setting and at the community level, so that those making the decisions about programs will be more fully informed of what contributes to success and so more potent health behavior programs are implemented.

Last, the process presented in this book is important because it is guided by research, theory, and practice. Models for particular behaviors in a given community with a specified group of young people are created, and these models drive the development of the community-wide programs. These models also provide the templates for evaluation so that the program developer can assess what worked in creating changes that are observed. The models can then be revised to guide the development of subsequent programs—the most potent aspects of the programs can be retained and disseminated. Thus, the process of developing health behavior programs becomes cyclical, guided by research, theory, and practice and enriched with experience and data from the community.

SUCCESSFUL HEALTH BEHAVIOR CHANGE PROGRAMS

The following are brief summaries of successful health behavior change programs with children and adolescents. These programs are part of research trials for which I served either as principal investigator or as an active collaborator. These are clearly not the only successful programs in children's health behavior change, but because they are the ones with which I'm most familiar and because they have all been derived from similar models, they form the basis of the process that will be described. These successful programs will serve as guides and models throughout the book. A "successful" program is one that demonstrates change in the targeted behavior or behaviors of children and adolescents as part of a controlled research trial. A discussion of research design and evaluation methods is beyond the scope of this book, but the reader is referred to Murray (1998) for a comprehensive discussion of outcome evaluation methods for community trials.

It is important to note that until the mid-1970s, there were no documented community-wide health behavior programs that had been successful in changing the behavior of a large number of children and adolescents. For example, despite the landmark 1964 Surgeon General's Report and widespread dissemination of information on the harmful consequences of smoking, adolescents continued to initiate smoking during the 1960s and 1970s (USDHHS, 1994). In fact, adolescent females significantly increased their smoking during this period, an increase that has been shown to be associated with the introduction of female brands of cigarettes (Pierce, Lee, & Gilpin, 1994). In addition, multiple research studies that evaluated new and existing school-based efforts to prevent the onset of smoking had not found any successful programs. The introduction of a new approach to smoking prevention, one guided by behavioral theories, was a significant breakthrough in health behavior change programs, when consistent reductions in the onset of smoking among young adolescents were achieved (USDHHS, 1994). A similar story could be told for other health behaviors of interest—eating patterns, physical activity, alcohol and drug use, and so on. Successful programs in these areas have emerged in only the past 15 to 20 years. Therefore, the programs described in this book are important in demonstrating that behavior change among large groups of young people is possible but challenging—and has only recently been achieved.

The Minnesota Heart Health Program: The Class of 1989 Study

The Minnesota Heart Health Program (MHHP) was a community-based heart disease prevention program funded by the National Heart, Lung, and

Blood Institutes from 1980 to 1993. MHHP was a research and demonstration project with the goal of reducing heart disease in three north-central U.S. communities compared with three matched reference communities in the same region (Blackburn et al., 1984). The intervention program consisted of risk factor screening and follow-up, community organization, direct adult education, environmental changes, health professional education, and mass media and youth education (Mittelmark et al., 1986). Evaluation of the impact of MHHP on adults is presented elsewhere (Luepker et al., 1994).

Youth education consisted of school-based health behavior programs in the classrooms, parental involvement, and youth participation in the adult components of MHHP (Perry, Klepp, & Sillers, 1989). The Class of 1989 Study was designed to evaluate the impact of the MHHP youth education efforts in one of the communities, Fargo (North Dakota)-Moorehead (Minnesota), compared with the reference community, Sioux Falls (South Dakota) (Perry, Klepp, et al., 1989). Students in both communities were surveyed annually, beginning in 1983, when they were in 6th grade, to 1989, when they were in 12th grade. In addition, students in Fargo-Moorehead participated in five years of behavioral health curricula in their classrooms from 1983 through 1987, while they were in 6th through 10th grades, and were exposed to and participated in the community-wide activities of MHHP, including risk factor screening, mass media campaigns, grocery story and restaurant labelling of healthy foods, and quit-smoking contests.

Each of the youth education programs was developed based on a theoretical model that was derived from problem behavior and social learning theories (Bandura, 1977; Jessor & Jessor, 1977; Perry & Jessor, 1985). The primary goal of the Class of 1989 intervention was cardiovascular health promotion; behavioral objectives included smoking reduction, adoption of a low-fat, low-sodium dietary pattern, and increasing regular physical activity. The programs introduced healthy role models through the use of same-age peer leaders, provided skills training in how to perform these healthier behaviors, created the norm of a healthy lifestyle, and provided incentives and reinforcement for participation and behavior changes. In each year, a particular behavior was emphasized, such as eating patterns in the 6th and 10th grades, cigarette smoking in the 7th and 9th grades, and physical activity in the 8th and 10th grades. In addition, alcohol and drug use was addressed in the 9th-grade curriculum. This allowed sufficient time to provide clear behavioral messages, skills training, rehearsal, and reinforcement concerning each behavior.

The results of the Class of 1989 have been published elsewhere (Kelder, Perry, & Klepp, 1993; Kelder, Perry, Lytle, & Klepp, 1993; Klepp, Kelder, & Perry, 1995; Perry, Kelder, & Klepp, 1994a; Perry, Kelder, Murray, & Klepp, 1992). Significant improvements in cardiovascular health behaviors were achieved. Students in Fargo-Moorhead, at the end of high school, were 40% less likely to be smoking cigarettes than same-age students in Sioux Falls. They were also more likely to be choosing healthier foods and exercising regularly. The smoking prevention results are particularly notable. The same classroom-based smoking prevention program that was implemented in the Class of 1989 Study had, in a prior study independent of MHHP, demonstrated smoking reductions only up through 9th or 10th grades (Murray, Pirie, Luepker, & Pallonen, 1989). In MHHP, with the addition of a 9th-grade booster curriculum and community components (mass media, quit contests, encouragement for adults to stop smoking), significant decreases in onset persisted until high school graduation (Perry, Kelder, et al., 1992).

The Child and Adolescent Trial for Cardiovascular Health (CATCH)

CATCH was a school-based community trial in four sites, funded by the National Heart, Lung and Blood Institutes, and implemented in three phases from 1987 to 1998. The goals of the trial were to reduce cardiovascular risk factors (cholesterol, blood pressure) and risk behaviors (dietary fat intake, sedentary behavior, smoking onset) among a cohort of students in their third, fourth, and fifth grades in school. The research design involved 96 schools, with 24 schools at each of four sites—California, Louisiana, Minnesota, and Texas. The 96 schools were randomly assigned (within each site) to one of three conditions: control (40 schools); school-based intervention (28 schools); school-based and family-based intervention (28 schools).

The intervention was based on prior work of the investigators and consisted of classroom-based behavioral curricula during the third through

Add: - Skill-training
-goal setting
- implementation surveys

fifth grades, changes in the choices in the school breakfast and lunch programs to be lower in fat and sodium, and changes in the physical education (PE) classes to include more moderate-to-vigorous physical activity for the students (Perry, Parcel, et al., 1992). In addition, in the school-based and family-based condition, students participated in take-home activities with their parents and were exposed to family fun nights with a heart health theme. The materials were developed to be appropriate to each grade level, as well as the multiple racial and ethnic groups in the study, and were translated into Spanish as needed.

Intervention development was based on social cognitive theory (Bandura, 1986) and included targeting changes in students' skills to select and eat healthier foods; skills to include physical activity in their daily lives; skills to resist influences to smoke; opportunities to eat healthier foods, exercise, and not smoke; and goal setting and reinforcements for behavior change (Perry, Stone, et al., 1990).

CATCH resulted in significant changes in the food provided by school lunches with the total fat and saturated fat content significantly reduced (Luepker et al., 1996). The physical education classes significantly increased the number of minutes that the children participated in vigorous physical activity (McKenzie et al., 1996). Self-reported dietary intake, measured by 24-hour food recalls, also showed significantly reduced fat intake (Lytle et al., 1996). Students in the intervention schools also increased their daily vigorous physical activity levels (Luepker et al., 1996). No additional changes were noted for the students who also received the parent intervention, and no significant effects of CATCH on any of the risk factors or for cigarette smoking onset were detected (Elder et al., 1996; Nader et al., 1996). High adherence to the study design and intervention programs was also noted (Perry et al., 1997).

The description and results of CATCH are presented in detail in numerous articles (Edmundson et al., 1996; Lytle et al., 1996; Nader et al., 1996; Perry, Parcel, et al., 1992; Stone et al., 1996), including the main outcome paper (Luepker et al., 1996). CATCH is notable because the changes in the school environment persisted over the 3 school years of the intervention and the behavioral changes have persisted for 6 years, up through at least 8th grade (Nader et al., in press). CATCH was able to sustain behavior changes beyond what the investigators had noted in their prior work, which had formed the basis of CATCH (Ellison, Capper, Goldberg, Witschi, & Stare, 1989; Perry, Luepker, et al., 1989; Simons-Morton, Parcel, & O'Hara, 1988). However, the lack of impact of the family component differed from previous findings (Nader et al., 1989; Perry et al., 1988) and suggests that programs aimed at changes in the family may need to be more intensive than what was offered with CATCH.

The Five-A-Day Power Plus Study

The Five-A-Day Power Plus Study (Power Plus) was a collaboration of researchers at the Minnesota Department of Health and the University of Minnesota, funded by the National Cancer Institute from 1992 to 1998. The goal of Power Plus was to increase fruit and vegetable consumption among fourth-grade and fifth-grade students in 20 elementary schools in Saint Paul, Minnesota, a large, urban school district. The schools were randomly assigned to intervention or delayed program condition. Students in the intervention schools participated in 2 school years of behavioral curricula, parental involvement programs, and school cafeteria changes to encourage eating more fruits and vegetables ("5 servings a day"). Schools in the delayed program condition received materials and training for the program after the final data had been collected.

The classroom curricula were written with colorful cartoon characters and included self-monitoring of fruits and vegetables eaten at lunch, group competitions, incentives, and rewards. The parental involvement program included suggested activities, information on increasing fruit and vegetable consumption at home, and "snack packs" that contained the ingredients (including produce) to prepare a fruit or vegetable snack for the family. The investigators worked with the school cafeteria personnel to ensure more choices of fruits and vegetables, extra servings, and appealing recipes to encourage more selection of fruits and vegetables at school lunch.

Power Plus was effective in significantly increasing total fruit consumption of the students and total fruits and vegetables at lunch (Perry et al., 1998). Significant changes in vegetable consumption were observed only among girls at lunch. Thus, Power Plus, a very targeted program, was able to achieve changes in fruit and vegetable consumption, primarily at lunch. A more extensive family involvement program and greater attention to making vegetables more appealing might have strengthened the interven-

behavioral interventions are not easily generalizable across multiple behaviors need to be quite specific

tion. It is of interest to note that CATCH, which encouraged a healthy diet, including fruits and vegetables but targeting higher fat foods, was able to create changes in fat consumption among the students, but no overall changes in fruit and vegetable consumption were found (Perry, Lytle, et al., 1998). This suggests that behavioral interventions are not easily generalizable across multiple behaviors and need to be quite specific concerning the behaviors that are being targeted, with sufficient time and reinforcement allocated to changing those behaviors.

The World Health Organization Study of Alcohol Education in Four Countries

WHO: comparison, peer-led groups

The World Health Organization (WHO) sponsored a pilot study of alcohol education among eighth-grade students in 25 schools in four countries: Australia (6 schools), Chile (3 schools), Norway (14 schools), and Swaziland (2 schools) from 1985 to 1987. The alcohol education program was classroom based and involved five classroom sessions over 2 months. Schools within each country were randomly assigned to one of three conditions: control (6 schools); teacher-led alcohol education program (9 schools); peer-led alcohol education program (10 schools).

The alcohol education program was derived from the social influences model that was used in smoking prevention (Perry, Grant, et al., 1989; USDHHS, 1994). Students in this program learned about the negative short-term consequences of drinking, why young people their age begin to drink, social influences to drink from advertising and others, and skills to resist those influences. In the teacher-led condition, trained teachers taught the entire program, using large-group discussion methods. In the peer-led condition, selected or volunteer students were trained to conduct the same program, using small-group discussions led by a peer leader. The programs were the same in each country, although role-plays, scenarios, and language were appropriate to each site (Perry & Grant, 1991; Perry, Grant, et al., 1989).

Only students in the peer-led alcohol education program reduced their drinking, which was found in all four countries. Students in the teacher-led program drank as much as the controls, even though their knowledge levels had increased. Thus, this pilot study was important in demonstrating the potential for international dissemination and collaboration, as well as the potency of peer leaders, particularly during early adolescence and even in other countries (Perry & Grant, 1991; Perry, Grant, et al., 1989).

Project Northland

Project Northland was a community-wide program designed to reduce adolescent alcohol use and alcohol-related problems, funded by the National Institute on Alcoholism and Alcohol Abuse. It was implemented in 24 school districts and adjoining communities from 1991 to 1998, targeting the Class of 1998 cohort. School districts were blocked by size in 1991 and randomized to intervention and delayed program conditions. Project Northland was divided into two phases. Phase I was when the cohort was in early adolescence, in their 6th, 7th, and 8th grade years in school; Phase II was when the cohort was in high school, in their 11th and 12th grade years (Komro, Perry, Williams, et al., in press; Perry, Williams, et al., 1993). During Phase I, the emphasis was on reducing demand for alcohol use among young adolescents. Phase II focused on reducing the supply of alcohol to teens.

The Project Northland interventions consisted of school-based curricula, parental involvement and education programs, peer leadership opportunities, community task forces and action teams, and a mass media campaign (Komro, Perry, et al., 1996; Perry et al., 1996; Veblen-Mortenson et al., 1999; Williams & Perry, 1998). Each year, an intervention was created that was relevant to the developmental stage of the cohort, thereby providing a theme for the entire year. For example, the 6th-grade program centered around the adventures of Slick Tracy and Breathtest Mahoney (cartoon characters and booklets created for Project Northland) with a peer-led classroom-based program, a set of home-based activity packets, and a Slick Tracy Night for students, parents, and community members (Williams et al., 1995).

At this writing, Phase II outcome data are currently being collected and processed and are not yet available. At the end of Phase I, when students were in 8th grade, there were significant reductions in drinking among students in the intervention communities (Perry et al., 1996). Students reduced their past-month alcohol use by 20% and past-week use by 30%. In addition, use of both cigarettes and alcohol was significantly reduced. Reductions in cigarette smoking, alcohol, and marijuana use were particularly notable among those who had not used alcohol at baseline, at the beginning of 6th grade. The project also affected Minnesota Multiphasic Personality Inventory-Adolescent (MMPI-A) scales that had been developed to assess clinical problems related to adolescents' alcohol and other drug use (Williams, Butcher, Ben-Porath, & Graham, 1992; Williams, Perry, Farbakhsh, & Veblen-Mortenson, 1999). The changes were attributable to changes in peer influences, peer norms, parent-child communication, the functional meanings of alcohol use, and self-efficacy to refuse alcohol at a party. Project Northland, therefore, demonstrates the feasibility of implementing a multiyear, multicomponent, community-wide intervention.

Summary of Programs

A summary of these five health behavior research programs for children and adolescents is shown in Table 1.1.

It should be noted that all of these programs were funded by grants from the National Institutes of Health, the WHO, or from private foundations. The scope of these programs—in terms of the number of program components and years of implementation—may therefore be greater than what is usually feasible for community groups. There are many resources for outside funding of programs for youth, and the process described in this book may serve to clarify goals, intervention objectives, and program components that will make grants more appealing to funding agencies. The process should also help make better use of limited resources.

The process described in this book is not guaranteed to be 100% successful, despite the outcomes noted above. However, following the process should increase the likelihood of success and of finding the causes of an unsuccessful program. These issues are discussed in the last chapter.

A BROAD VIEW OF HEALTH

The programs described in the foregoing discussion focused on particular behaviors of children and adolescents—cigarette smoking, fat and salt intake, fruit and vegetable consumption, physical activity, and alcohol use. A variety of health-compromising behaviors of children and adolescents, in addition to these, are also of great concern. Violence, the use of drugs,

TABLE 1.1   Summary of Research Studies of Health Behavior Change
With Children and Adolescents

Study	Behavioral Objectives	Population	Intervention	Outcomes
Class of 1989 Study	Improve eating and activity patterns; prevent smoking; reduce alcohol and marijuana use	Two north-central communities; middle class, white; 6th to 12th grades; $N = 2,401$	Behavioral health curricula for 5 years; Fargo-Moorhead Heart Health Program for 6 years	Reduced smoking rates; greater physical activity; improved food choices; short-term reductions in alcohol, marijuana use
CATCH	Decrease fat in diet; increase physical activity, decrease fat in school food; increase vigorous activity in PE; achieve smoke-free schools	Ninety-six schools in four states; Multiethnic-multiracial groups; 3rd to 5th grades; $N = 7,795$	Behavioral health curricula for 3 years; parental involvement; school food service changes; PE changes; smoking policies	Decreased saturated fat, total fat in diet; decreased fat in school food served; increased vigorous activity; increased activity in PE
Power Plus	Increase fruit and vegetable intake at lunch and all day	Twenty schools in St. Paul, Minnesota; Multiethnic-multiracial groups; 4th and 5th grades; $N = 1,750$	Behavioral health curricula for 2 years; parental involvement; school food service involvement	Increased fruit and vegetables at lunch; increased fruit intake all day; increased vegetables at lunch for females
WHO Study	Decrease alcohol use	Four countries: Australia, Chile, Norway, Swaziland, 8th grade; $N = 2,497$	Behavioral health curricula for 3 months; peer leaders in one third of the schools	Decreased alcohol use in peer-led program
Project Northland	Decrease alcohol use	Twenty-four school districts and 28 communities in northeastern Minnesota; middle class, white; 6th to 8th grades; $N = 2,351$	Behavioral health curricula for 3 years; peer leadership; parental involvement; community task forces	Decreased alcohol use at end of 3 years during early adolescence; decreased smoking and marijuana use among baseline nonusers

precocious or unprotected sexual behavior, obesity, and teenage pregnancy all rank as health problems of children and adolescents in the United States (Carnegie Council on Adolescent Development, 1992; Dryfoos, 1998; Ozer, Brindis, Millstein, Knopt, & Irwin, 1998). All of these behaviors have been shown to significantly compromise health. For example, almost all cigarette smoking begins during adolescence, with 1 out of 3 teen smokers projected to die prematurely because of their smoking (Centers for Disease Control and Prevention [CDC], 1996b; USDHHS, 1994). Alcohol use is the behavior associated with the greatest number of deaths during adolescence (Komro, Hu, & Flay, 1997; Perry, Williams, et al., 1993). Dietary behaviors, which are learned in childhood and appear to track during adolescence (Kelder, Perry, Klepp, & Lytle, 1994), are the second leading cause of cancer (World Cancer Research Fund, 1997).

Health is, however, more than the prevention of premature death or the absence of disease or infirmity. Health is a dynamic state of complete physical, psychological, spiritual, and social well-being (Nutbeam, 1997; Perry & Jessor, 1985). Physical health refers to physical or physiological functioning. Psychological health considers an individual's subjective sense of well-being, such as not being depressed, as well as conforming to society's standards of behavior (e.g., not being sociopathic or conduct disordered). Spiritual health involves the incorporation of a higher or transcendent purpose to existence. Social health implies the satisfactory fulfillment of one's social roles (son, daughter, student, church member, spouse, worker, etc.). Therefore, behaviors that compromise health are not only those that inflict physical pain, disease, or death but also those that affect one's social, psychological, or spiritual well-being.

This broader conceptualization of health may be particularly important in the health behaviors of children and adolescents. First, the outcomes of high-risk behaviors may first manifest in these other domains of health. For example, students who are experimenting with alcohol may first be detected at school and receive disciplinary action. This is a social consequence of alcohol use, which compromises their role as student. Because it may occur early in the experimental phase of drinking, it may also be an opportunity for early intervention, before physical harm takes place. Second, the physical outcomes may be secondary to problems in other domains. Adolescents with low self-images, for example, are more likely to try to compensate by adopting a new image, such as by smoking cigarettes

(USDHHS, 1994). Suicide can be a result of undetected mental health problems, such as depression (Moscicki, 1995; Reinherz et al., 1995). Each domain of health needs to be considered in a health behavior program so the program is health-promoting for all of the domains. This also creates greater potential for effectiveness, because the various domains of health reinforce each other.

Health behavior programs for youth are part of the more comprehensive purview of health promotion, the process of enabling people to increase control over, and to improve, their health (WHO, 1986). According to the Ottawa Charter for Health Promotion, the fundamental conditions for health are peace, shelter, education, food, income, a stable ecosystem, sustainable resources, social justice, and equity. Health promotion involves building healthy public policies, creating supportive environments, strengthening community action, developing personal skills, and reorienting health services (WHO, 1986). Thus, the development of health behavior programs takes place within this broader framework, acknowledging the importance of larger social and political issues that affect health and recognizing this more comprehensive view of what it means to promote health.

THE CHALLENGE

This book, then, has the challenge of providing a description of a process that will lead to the development of more effective health behavior programs for children and adolescents in our communities, that is, programs that will result in increased health-enhancing behaviors among the targeted population of youth. The process of program development in our own work has consisted of 10 steps. The 10 steps are shown in Table 1.2.

Each of the steps is discussed in the following chapters, guided by key questions for each of the steps. The steps are presented as a linear, progressive process. In reality, this is not always the case, and the process may be more of a spiral, with some of the steps repeated as necessary. These steps will be discussed in four primary stages: preparing for program development (Chapter 2); determining the program components (Chapter 3); creating the health behavior program (Chapter 4); and implementing and maintaining a program (Chapter 5). Each of these stages will be discussed

TABLE 1.2 Developing Health Behavior Programs: Ten Steps

Study	*Behavioral Objectives*
Step 1:	Selecting health behaviors for a community-wide program
Step 2:	Providing a rationale for selecting a health behavior
Step 3:	Creating an intervention model of predictive factors
Step 4:	Writing the intervention objectives
Step 5:	Ensuring that the intervention objectives are applicable to the targeted population
Step 6:	Determining which types of programs are most applicable
Step 7:	Creating program components from intervention objectives
Step 8:	Constructing the health behavior program
Step 9:	Implementing community-wide health behavior programs
Step 10:	Maintaining health behavior programs

with examples from the programs already discussed, as applicable. The intent, then, of this book is to provide steps for developing programs that will lead to meaningful change in improving the health behavior of young people, in the broader context of improving physical, psychological, social, and spiritual well-being.

The book focuses on the behavior of whole communities of young people. As such, program development includes both individual behavior change and environmental change approaches. This process also incorporates a youth development perspective because it not only identifies risk factors for given problem behaviors, but a range is given of predictive factors at the community level that are associated with health-related behaviors of young people and that facilitate their healthful development (Saito, Benson, Blyth, & Sharma, 1995).

Given this process and the 10 steps, it is up to program developers to decide the needs and constraints of their communities, to focus on a specific behavior or behaviors, and to specify program goals and anticipated outcomes. It is my hope that the book will provide the map, guidelines, and tools for these efforts.

2

PREPARING FOR PROGRAM DEVELOPMENT

This chapter discusses the first three steps in program development. These steps involve selecting and analyzing the behavior that is the focus of the program and creating an intervention model. The behavior or behaviors to be targeted by a program are often mandated by funding agencies or community leaders rather than selected by the program developer, and the specifics of the behavior are often not well defined. This chapter provides guidelines on how to determine the appropriateness of the behavior to target, how to define and limit the behaviors for a program, and how to identify a target group. For a health behavior program to be successful with young people, it is critical to know what outcome is sought (in terms of behavior change) and for whom.

STEP 1: SELECTING HEALTH BEHAVIORS FOR A COMMUNITY-WIDE PROGRAM

Selection of a health behavior is the first of 10 steps in program development. Often, the behavior is selected for, rather than by, the program developer—through an expressed need of a community or by a funding agency. There is a need to narrow the scope of a health behavior program to a specific behavior or behaviors in order to achieve change, because each health behavior is regulated by a different set of predictive factors. What are the criteria for selecting a health behavior or behaviors for a community-wide program? The criteria used are analogous to defining a public health problem that warrants a public health response, because these programs are aimed at whole communities rather than individuals. Generally, there are

17

TABLE 2.1   Step 1: Selecting Health Behaviors for a Community-Wide Program

The following questions provide a framework for deciding whether a given health behavior is appropriate as the focus of a community-wide program:

1. Is the behavior health compromising? How does it affect the multiple domains of young people's health?
2. Is the behavior a community-wide problem? That is, do a large number of children and adolescents engage in the behavior, rather than a small subgroup? Is it persistent over time? Does it have the potential to spread?
3. Are the behaviors part of the public domain? Are potential solutions possible at the community level? Will the community support a large-scale effort?

three major types of questions that are addressed in determining whether a given health behavior is appropriate for a community-wide program. These are shown in Table 2.1.

The health behaviors of greatest interest are those that are health-compromising, especially across multiple domains of health. For example, adolescent alcohol and drug use can seriously affect physical health (i.e., car crashes), social health (school problems), psychological health (depression), and spiritual health (by limiting their range of interests). These behaviors are also those that are community-wide so that changes at the community level can make a difference. For example, cigarette smoking among young people is initiated and maintained, in part, due to advertising and promotional activities, access to cigarettes, and price. These factors need to be addressed at the community level, because they affect all young people within a given environment. If the problem is confined to just a few young people, then other types of programs are more appropriate. For example, because depressive behaviors have become widespread, a community-wide approach may be warranted (Depression Guideline Panel, 1993). However, other mental health problems, such as schizophrenia, may be too low in prevalence for a community-wide effort; other more individualized or group approaches might be more appropriate, efficient, and efficacious.

The health behaviors should also be persistent or likely to spread. A large-scale, multicomponent, community-wide effort is probably not warranted for a behavior that is not likely to last. This could be the case for body piercing or tattoos that are currently in vogue. However, unprotected sexual behaviors that can lead to HIV infection clearly have the potential to spread so that a large-scale effort is appropriate, a view that led to nationwide action by the Centers for Disease Control and Prevention. Last, the health behaviors need to be in the public domain to be able to reach the target audience with a community-wide program. For example, there are limitations on what can be done with children and adolescents within their homes, because their homes are not in the public domain, so a family-based health problem, such as abusive marital relationships, may be difficult to change through a community-wide program. Also, evidence that the community is "ready" for a program, or at least not opposed to the program, is needed. For example, antismoking activities, such as increased state excise taxes, have not been as readily adopted in tobacco-growing areas of the United States (USDHHS, 1994).

STEP 2: PROVIDING A RATIONALE FOR THE SELECTED HEALTH BEHAVIOR

The second step involves providing a rationale for the selected health behavior. This includes research and theory on the health behavior so that the program developer becomes an "expert" on that subject area. This examination not only provides grounding for the developer but also provides a check on the behavior selected (whether it is really appropriate for a community-wide program), whether the behavior is too broadly defined (because specificity results in better program outcomes), and the selection of appropriate target group(s).

In this step, it is helpful to start by answering three questions. These are shown in Table 2.2.

How Does the Behavior Compromise Health?

To address the first question, a literature review is required. The goal of the review is to defend the selected behavior as a public health problem that warrants a community-wide effort. The literature on most health behaviors is multidisciplinary, especially when a broad definition of health is applied, so that the medical, public health, sociological, psychological, educational, social work, and economics literatures (and maybe others) could contribute to such a review. To understand this literature and to be

TABLE 2.2   Step 2: Providing a Rationale for the Selected Health Behavior

The following three questions provide the framework for writing a rationale for the health behavior, defining the behavior, and selecting appropriate target groups:

1. What does research, theory, and scholarly work suggest are the consequences of the behavior in the physical, psychological, social, and spiritual domains of health? Are these short-term or long-term consequences?
2. What is the epidemiology of the behavior? How many people engage in the behavior? At what age? Are there gender, racial-ethnic group, or socioeconomic differences?
3. What is the etiology of the behavior? Why do young people engage in the behavior? What are the sociodemographic, social-environmental, personal, and behavioral factors that predict the onset or maintenance of the behavior?

able to present the consequences of the behavior in a knowledgeable and succinct way, is particularly important in initiating a program in the community.

A grid is useful in summarizing the literature and in encouraging thought about all the domains of health. The grid lists and defines the four domains of health on the left, and whether the behavior has short-term or long-term consequences for young people across the top. Generally, short-term consequences are those that occur during childhood and adolescence; they are immediate and may not be long lasting. Long-term consequences are those that manifest during adulthood and later in life but develop more slowly, even if their origins are in childhood. Table 2.3 provides an example of a grid on cigarette smoking among adolescents as a health-compromising behavior, with data from the 1994 Surgeon General's Report (SGR; USDHHS, 1994).

It is recommended that a grid be created for the selected health behavior and a short, one-page to two-page summary of the consequences of the health behavior be prepared, with the referenced literature attached. This provides the evidence that the behavior is important because it compromises the health of people in the short-term and long-term. It also provides various frames from which to view the behavior. For example, framing cigarette smoking as an addictive behavior during adolescence (not just during adulthood) has been important in convincing the public and policy makers that primary prevention with adolescents is critical to ameliorating this public health problem.

TABLE 2.3   Cigarette Smoking Among Adolescents as a
Health-Compromising Behavior[a]

	Short-Term Consequences	*Long-Term Consequences*
Physical health[b] (Physiological functioning, the absence of disease, wellness)	Lung functioning Athletic performance Respiratory illnesses	Cardiovascular disease Cancer #1 Cause of death: 400,000 deaths per year; 1 out of 3 teen smokers die prematurely
Psychological health (Perceptions of self, not being depressed, emotional functioning)	Addiction Depression Self-image Feelings of helplessness	Addiction Depression
Social health (Role fulfillment, acquiring skills, completing basic life tasks)	School performance Use of other drugs	Worksite performance Lost revenue from cost of cigarettes Social disapproval Societal cost of smoking
Spiritual health (A purpose to existence, transcendence, interests beyond status quo)	Limiting range of options and interests	"Slow motion suicide"

a. The consequences of smoking among adolescents come from the 1994 Surgeon General's Report (USDHHS, 1994).

b. The domains of health are discussed in Perry and Jessor (1985).

What Is the Epidemiology of the Behavior?

The next question on the epidemiology of the behavior requires the review of available data on the behavior. It is important to know the following:

- The percentage of children and adolescents who engage in the behavior
- The percentage of adults who engage in the behavior
- The age at which the behavior begins
- The percentage of young males versus young females who engage in the behavior
- The percentage of young people who engage in the behavior at particular ages or grade levels
- The percentage of young people of different racial or ethnic groups who engage in the behavior

- The percentage of young people from varying socioeconomic groups who engage in the behavior
- Whether the behavior is becoming more prevalent among young people, or for males or females, or within a given ethnic-racial or socioeconomic group
- If the behavior is more prevalent in urban, suburban, or rural settings

Reviewing data on the health behavior is critical to selecting a target group, that is, the young people who are most in need of a program or most critical for intervention. The selected target group should exhibit substantial prevalence of the behavior, or be at risk for increasing prevalence of the behavior, or be the group where the behavior is initiated. For example, the prevalence of cigarette smoking increases with age and grade levels in high school, so adolescents in high school might appear to be the optimal group for intervention because there are substantial numbers who smoke. However, smoking begins in early adolescence, so to reduce the onset of smoking, targeting middle school or junior high school students is needed, prior to addiction (USDHHS, 1994). Both genders and all racial-ethnic groups have increased their smoking rates in the 1990s, so all youth appear to "need" a health behavior program. In addition, interventions with young adolescents seem particularly crucial because that is the developmental stage when smoking is most appealing and when onset occurs (USDHHS, 1994). In smoking prevention, then, it is recommended to intervene with all youth populations, because all young people are at risk for smoking.

Fortunately, in addition to data on cigarette smoking, there are multiple national data bases available on child and adolescent health behaviors that are useful in examining the epidemiology of a given health behavior. These national data bases are described in a monograph titled *America's Adolescents: Are They Healthy?* from the University of California San Francisco (Ozer et al., 1997). The Centers for Disease Control sponsors the National Death Index, the Sexually Transmitted Disease Surveillance, the Youth Risk Behavior Surveillance System, the National Health Interview Survey, and the National Survey of Family Growth, which provide data on adolescent morbidity, mortality, and a variety of health risk behaviors (Ozer et al., 1997; see http://www.cdc.gov/scientific.htm). For example, the Youth Risk Behavior Surveillance System (YRBSS) was established to measure six categories of health behaviors among adolescents: (a) behaviors that contribute to unintentional and intentional injuries; (b) tobacco use; (c) alcohol and other drug use; (d) sexual behaviors that result in unintended pregnancy and sexually transmitted disease, including HIV infection; (e) dietary behaviors; and (f) physical activity. Data are collected biannually, through national, state, and local school-based surveys of high school students, grades 9 through 12, in all 50 states and the District of Columbia (Kann, Kolbe, & Collins, 1993; Kolbe, 1990). The surveys are anonymous to protect student privacy. Data from the YRBSS can be obtained through the Division of Adolescent and School Health at CDC or from the web site for the YRBSS: http://www.cdc.gov/ nccdphp/dash/yrbs/ov.htm.

For longitudinal trends on adolescent tobacco, alcohol, and drug use behaviors, the Monitoring the Future (MTF) study is an excellent source. This study is conducted by the Institute for Social Research at the University of Michigan and involves data collected annually on a nationally representative sample of high school seniors from 1975 to the present (Johnston, O'Malley, & Bachman, 1996). Since 1991, 8th-grade and 10th-grade students have also been surveyed. Data can be obtained from the investigators, who publish annual reports, or from the MTF web site at http://www.isr.umich.edu/src/mtf/. Considerable data are now available through the Internet, where recent data are often posted before written reports are disseminated.

Data that characterize young people in the local community or state or region are also important, as these data are seen as more relevant to constituents. State-level and some community-level data are available from the YRBSS. Local foundations, health agencies, state departments, and university researchers can also be called to find out what data are available relevant to a given behavior. In health behavior programs at the University of Minnesota, data reports are provided annually to the schools and communities in our research studies, regardless of whether they are part of the intervention or reference (control) groups. In surveying youth, we often use the same questions that are used in national surveys, such as the MTF survey, so that data from our schools and communities can be compared with state and national data. This is one of the benefits we can offer to schools and communities that collaborate with us. We have found that the more localized the data, the more likely it is that the data are perceived as important and meaningful—because they reveal the behavior of young people in their settings.

TABLE 2.4   Cigarette Smoking and Teens—Key Facts

1. Nearly 2.5 million teens try their first cigarette each year. Of those teens, 1 out of 3 will smoke daily before high school graduation.

2. Over 80% of people who ever smoke try their first cigarette before age 18.

3. Over 50% of people who smoke daily begin daily smoking between ages 12 to 17.

4. Four out of five teens who smoke daily as high school seniors will still be smoking 5 to 6 years later as adults.

5. One out of three teens who smoke will die prematurely due to their smoking.

6. Among high school seniors, 36.5% were current smokers in 1997. Males smoked slightly more than females. Caucasians smoked the most (40.7%), followed by Hispanics (25.9%), and African Americans (14.3%).

7. There have been significant increases in smoking among adolescents in the 1990s. This is true for both genders and all racial-ethnic groups. This is the first major increase in 25 years.

Once data are reviewed on a health behavior, then a summary report should be written. This report should be very clear about who is engaging in the behavior, when it starts, and whether there have been changes over time. This report can be succinct, but it is often useful to create a fact sheet related to the behavior that can be shared with community members when the health behavior program is being initiated. A sample fact sheet for adolescent cigarette smoking is shown in Table 2.4.

Why Do Young People Engage in the Behavior?

The etiology of a given behavior is the plausible and verifiable analysis of why the behavior occurs. It consists of a theory-guided set of factors that predict the behavior's onset and maintenance. Thus, to address the third question on etiology, a review of prior etiologic research and of theories of health behavior is needed. Theories of adolescent behavior and health behaviors serve as the framework for explaining why the behavior occurs. Reviews of prior etiologic research provide data as to which factors are predictive of the particular behavior. However, if data are limited or do not exist, then theories can be used to guide program development until more etiologic research has been done. The identification of predictive factors is crucial to the development of health behavior programs, because the most potent of these factors form the basis of these programs. The objective of

"The objective of health behavior programs is to change the predictive factors that serve to support and reinforce the targeted behavior

Health Behavior Program	➡	Changes in Predictive Factors	➡	Changes in Behavior

Figure 2.1.

health behavior programs is to change the predictive factors that serve to support and reinforce the targeted behavior. For example, because having peers who smoke is one of the predictive factors for smoking onset, an objective of a smoking prevention program might be to ameliorate this influence. Changing predictive factors should result in behavior change, as shown in Figure 2.1.

Although a thorough review of the etiologic research concerning a health behavior is required to understand the key factors that have been found to predict the onset and maintenance of a given behavior, there are particular factors that have been shown repeatedly to be predictive of young people's behavior and can be used as guides in this search.

Four sets of factors—sociodemographic, social-environmental, personal, and behavioral—form the basis of social learning theory (Bandura, 1977; Perry, Baranowski, & Parcel, 1990), social cognitive theory (Bandura, 1986; Baranowski, Perry, & Parcel, 1997), problem behavior theory (Jessor & Jessor, 1977), and theories of adolescent health behavior (Perry & Jessor, 1985). These sets of factors were used to design the health behavior programs described in Chapter 1 and are discussed more thoroughly for the Class of 1989 Study (Perry, Klepp, et al., 1989), CATCH (Perry, Stone, et al., 1990), Project Northland (Perry, Williams, et al., 1993), and the WHO Study on alcohol education (Perry, Grant, et al., 1989). An excellent resource on multiple theories of health behavior, their key constructs, examples of how they've been applied in health education programs, and their limitations is *Health Behavior and Health Education: Theory, Research, and Practice* (Glanz, Lewis, & Rimer, 1997).

Sociodemographic Factors

The key sociodemographic factors are those generally found in the epidemiologic analysis of the behavior, such as age, gender, racial-ethnic group, and urban-rural differences. There are also differences in behavior of young people due to socioeconomic levels, parental educational levels, and family structure (Montgomery, Kiely, & Pappas, 1996; Winkleby, Jatulis, Frank, & Fortmann, 1992). These are aspects of the larger society that, for the most part, cannot directly be addressed or changed in a health behavior program, as they are generally beyond the scope of a given program. However, they are critical in identifying a target group that may be at risk and in understanding the opportunities and constraints of that group (Resnicow, Braithwaite, & Kuo, 1997). Moreover, large inequities in the community or society that are associated with health outcomes need to be addressed through political processes and require our involvement both personally and professionally (Perry, 1998).

Social-Environmental Factors

The social-environmental factors are of primary importance in the development of health behavior programs for children and adolescents. These factors have been repeatedly among the most powerful in explaining young people's behavior (Jessor & Jessor, 1977; Resnick et al., 1997; Roski et al., 1997; USDHHS, 1994) and in instigating behavior change (Perry et al., 1996). Figure 2.2 presents a drawing of the social environment of young people. The young person is at the middle of his or her social environment, with the closest influences generally being parents, siblings and best friends, and those influences further away being community policies and practices, advertising and promotional activities, mass media, and societal leaders.

There is ample evidence that all levels of the social environment directly affect the behavior of young people (Roski et al., 1997) and emerging evidence of the powerful influence of the outer levels. For example, among never-smoking, not-susceptible adolescents, those who had a favorite cigarette advertisement were 2 times as likely to make the transition to smoking after 3 years, compared with those who did not have a favorite cigarette advertisement (Pierce, Choi, Gilpin, Farkas, & Berry, 1998). Young people who said they would use a cigarette promotional item, such as a cap or jacket, were 3 times more likely to make the transition to smoking. Having peers or parents who smoke, which traditionally are found to be predictive of the transition to smoking, were not found to be predictive (Pierce et al., 1998). This study, then, demonstrates how all

Social environmental influence that people think of key theoretical factors
- normative Expectations
- role models
- opportunities
- social support

Preparing for Program Development   27

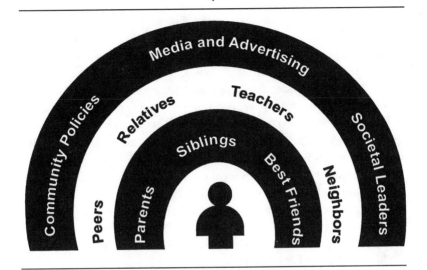

Figure 2.2. The Social Environment of Young People

levels of the social environment may affect young people's behavior, such as the initiation of smoking, and the relative potency of those factors in the outer ring.

Each level of the social environment shown in Figure 2.2 influences young people through four key theoretical factors: normative expectations, role models, opportunities, and social support (Perry & Jessor, 1985; Perry, Kelder, & Komro, 1993; Roski et al., 1997). These are major factors that have been shown to predict young people's behavior and can be changed by intervention. Because of their potency, they warrant considerable consideration when creating a model of predictive factors for program development.

Normative expectations can be defined as what people perceive that they ought to do, what is acceptable behavior, and what others are doing (Baranowski, Perry, & Parcel, 1997; Montano, Kasprzyk, & Taplin, 1997; Roski et al., 1997). For example, adolescents greatly overestimate the number of adults and people their age who smoke (USDHHS, 1994); the greater the overestimation, the more likely it is that they will smoke in the future. This overestimating has been shown to be associated with exposure to cigarette advertising (USDHHS, 1994). The behavior of role models and

"Peer influence, such as best friend's behavior, is among the most powerful factor in predicting young adolescent behavior"

28   CREATING HEALTH BEHAVIOR CHANGE

the consequences of that behavior also influence young people's behavior (Bandura, 1977). Peer influence, such as a best friend's behavior, is among the most powerful factors in predicting young adolescent behavior (Perry, Williams, et al., 1993; USDHHS, 1994), because of the high value the young adolescent places on peers (Hill & Holmbeck, 1986). However, community norms appear to be equally as powerful as role models (Hansen & Graham, 1991; Roski et al., 1997). In a recent etiologic study of eighth-grade students' alcohol use, school and community norms and role models accounted for 38% to 53% of the variance in alcohol use, using scales that were derived from multiple levels of the social environment (Roski et al., 1997). Norms alone accounted for 33% to 38% of the variance.

The third social environmental factor, opportunities, considers whether the behavior is possible (Perry & Jessor, 1985; Wagenaar & Perry, 1994). Opportunities include the physical environment, such as whether smoking is allowed on school grounds, or physical education facilities are available, or whether lower fat foods are served at home. They also include the policies and practices of the community and its institutions, such as how easy it is for young people to have access to alcohol at community events, or whether sex education is taught at school, or whether cigarettes are expensive. This concept also includes lack of opportunities—barriers to engaging in health-compromising behaviors, such as through enforcement of policies at school and in the community. The final key environmental factor is social support, that is, whether others encourage the young person to engage in the behavior and whether young people generally perceive that they have a supportive environment, such as support and approval from parents and other significant adults (Heaney & Israel, 1997; USDHHS, 1994).

These four social environmental factors provide an important framework for examining the levels of the social environment. A chart that has the various levels of the social environment, and the theoretical factors, is useful for reviewing the etiologic literature. The chart shown in Table 2.5 provides a checklist of the literature on social environmental predictors that have consistently been shown to be related to adolescent smoking (Conrad, Flay, & Hill, 1992; USDHHS, 1994). From this chart, it can be seen that to make changes in key social environmental factors related to adolescent smoking, a multicomponent, community-wide program is needed, because so many levels of the social environment significantly contribute to each

TABLE 2.5 Social Environmental Factors Consistently Identified in Etiologic Research on Adolescent Smoking Onset

	Role Models (Others' behavior and consequences)	Norms (Expected, usual behavior)	Opportunities- Barriers (Potential to engage in behavior)	Social Support (Reinforcement)
Family members:				
Parents		X	X	X
Siblings	X			
Friends:				
Peers	X	X	X	X
Best friend	X	X		
Community:				
School		X	X	X
Community members		X		
Culture:				
Advertising	X	X		
Promotions	X		X	
Policies		X	X	

SOURCE: Conrad et al. (1992), USDHHS (1994).

factor. The checklist also shows to whom intervention might be directed, such as to parents, peers, and advertising as role models.

Personal Factors

The third set of factors are personal factors—factors inherent to individuals or groups of individuals that reside within the person and manifest as individual differences in a given environment (Perry & Jessor, 1985). The predominant personal factors that have been found to be predictive of health behaviors of youth include knowledge levels, values, functional meanings, self-image, and self-efficacy. Knowledge that is predictive of a behavior is generally specifically related to that behavior. This type of knowledge has been labelled "behavioral capability" (Baranowski et al., 1997). Thus, young people may have knowledge of the long-term health consequences of smoking, yet this knowledge will make little difference in changing the smoking onset process (USDHHS, 1994). However, knowledge of the social influences to begin to smoke and ways to identify and resist those influences are more proximal to the behavior and more predictive. Values refer to the relative importance placed on engaging in the behavior compared with other behaviors or other aspects of the young person's life (Strecher & Rosenstock, 1997). For example, a young person may take a drink of alcohol from a friend, even when not wanting to drink, because she or he places a high value on conformity with friends (Jessor & Jessor, 1977). Functional meanings are the functions that a behavior serves to the individual. This is similar to outcome expectations and the subjective expected utility of a behavior (Baranowski et al., 1997; Bauman & Fisher, 1985; USDHHS, 1994). Adolescents smoke, in part, because smoking is perceived as functional to them as a way to fit in, act maturely, assert their independence, or gain a new self-image (Perry, Murray, & Klepp, 1987). Self-image is a person's self-perception, generally of his or her external appearance. Those perceptions may include an ideal self-image (what one would like to be) or real self-image (one's actual perceptions of self; Chassin, Presson, & Sherman, 1990). Low self-images (relative to peers) and large discrepancies between ideal and real self-images are associated with increases in health-compromising behaviors, such as cigarette smoking, which may be seen as a way to improve one's self-image (USDHHS, 1994). Self-efficacy is the confidence to engage (or not engage) in a specific behavior (Bandura, 1977, 1995). Adolescents in the WHO study were quite confident that they could say "no" to alcohol at a religious activity but not very confident if it was offered to them by someone attractive of the opposite sex. Thus, self-efficacy can predict how likely the behavior will occur and under what circumstances.

Behavioral Factors

Behavioral factors are those directly associated with the enactment of the behavior (Perry & Jessor, 1985). These factors include behavioral intentions, other related behaviors, skills, and incentives.

Behavioral intentions include a young person's statements about the future (Montano et al., 1997), such as whether she or he will ever try a cigarette, eat broccoli, exercise regularly, watch less TV, and so on. When these intentions are specific and have a short time frame, they are quite powerful predictors of future behavior (Fishbein & Ajzen, 1975). In smoking research, for example, behavioral intentions have been used as a proxy for actual behavior among preteens, prior to the time of onset (USDHHS, 1994). Behaviors do not occur in isolation of each other, and engaging in one behavior may be strongly associated with others. Among adolescents, for example, problem behaviors occur as a syndrome, that is, the same adolescents may engage in multiple problem behaviors (Jessor & Jessor, 1977). Tobacco and alcohol use have been labelled as "gateway drugs" because they predict other drug use, such as marijuana use, but generally are initiated before other drug use (USDHHS, 1994). The reduction of alcohol use was the goal of Project Northland (Perry, Williams, et al., 1993), but the adolescents reduced both their alcohol and tobacco use as a result of the first 3 years of health behavior programs (Perry et al., 1996). Significant associations have also been observed between eating patterns, physical activity, and smoking prevalence (Lytle, Kelder, Perry, & Klepp, 1995). In developing a health behavior program, it is important to recognize the covariation of behaviors, because other behaviors may also need to be addressed if the program is to be successful (Lytle & Roski, 1997).

Skills are the third behavioral factor—the behavioral tools needed to enact a behavior. To eat more vegetables, for example, young people need to be able to select and prepare vegetables or ask their parents or guardians to purchase and serve vegetables. To avoid influences to smoke, young people need to be able to resist those influences, such as refusing offers from peers or counterarguing the messages in cigarette advertising and promotional activities (USDHHS, 1994). Thus, it is important to break down the behavior into the skills needed to engage (or not engage) in the behavior, as those will be a key part of a health behavior change program (Prochaska, Redding, & Evers, 1997).

Last, behaviors are more likely to be attempted if there are incentives and more likely to be repeated if there are rewards (Baranowski et al., 1997). There are many incentives and rewards for a young person to begin and continue to smoke—recognition from friends, acceptance into a peer group, attainment of promotional items from the tobacco industry (Schooler, Feighery, & Flora, 1996; USDHHS, 1994). Sometimes, incentives to engage in health-enhancing behaviors are not tangible or immediate. For example, for someone beginning a physical activity program, an already busy schedule may provide more disincentives than incentives.

TABLE 2.6   Summary of Major Factors Predictive of Young People's
                Health Behaviors

Sociodemographic Factors	
Age	Years, grade level, developmental stage
Gender	Male, female
Racial-ethnic group	Types of groups, mixed groups
Socioeconomic status	Poverty, unemployment
Urbanicity	Large metropolitan, urban, suburban, rural
Family composition	Parents, guardians, siblings, other relatives

Social Environmental Factors	
Normative expectations	Perceived usual or accepted behavior
Role models	Behavior of others and consequences
Opportunities-barriers	Possibility of engaging in the behavior
Social support	Social reinforcement from others

Personal Factors	
Behavioral capability	Knowledge of what is needed to behave
Values	Relative importance of the behavior
Functional meanings	The function the behavior serves
Self-image	Perceptions of self; ideal vs. real
Self-efficacy	Confidence to enact behavior

Behavioral Factors	
Behavioral intentions	Expected behavior in the future
Behavior repertoire	Related behaviors
Skills	Other behaviors needed to enact targeted behavior
Incentives-rewards	Tangible benefits of behavior

Finding potential incentives and rewards for health-enhancing behaviors
and diminishing those that support health-compromising behaviors may be
critical to the success of the health behavior program. These incentives
provide a source of motivation and compliance that is needed to balance
the rewards that already exist (Baranowski et al., 1997).

The sociodemographic, social environmental, personal, and behavioral
factors just discussed can provide a framework for establishing the etiology of a given behavior, because these have shown to be predictive for a
variety of behaviors and settings and useful in the development of health
behavior programs (Glanz et al., 1997). A summary of these factors is given
in Table 2.6.

Theoretical Factors and Etiologic Research

For each of the factors in Table 2.6, the following questions should be addressed:

- How does this factor relate to the behavior of interest? For example, which norms govern that behavior? What are the functional meanings of that behavior to young people? What skills are needed to enact that behavior?
- What does the etiologic research literature reveal about these factors? Have any of the factors been found to be predictive or not predictive? Which are most potent, that is, repeatedly been shown to be significantly predictive?
- What other factors are in the etiologic research literature that are predictive of the behavior? Can they be added to the sets of sociodemographic, social environmental, personal, and behavioral factors?

To address these questions, careful review of the etiologic research and analyses of the targeted behavior are needed. Because the program developer should be able to apply these theoretical factors in creating a health behavior program, particularly if the etiologic literature is lacking, thought and discussion of each factor and how it relates to the targeted behavior are crucial. These factors form the basis of program development. The program developer should prepare a listing of the major predictive factors for the behavior, definitions of those factors for the behavior, and an indication of which factors appear to be most predictive.

STEP 3: CREATING AN INTERVENTION MODEL OF PREDICTIVE FACTORS

An intervention model is used as the basis for program development; therefore, the model drives the health behavior program and its evaluation. Three questions are addressed in creating this model, as shown in Table 2.7.

The Target Group

The first question involves the identification of the targeted group. This is the group of young people for whom behavior change is sought. Like the targeted behavior, in many cases, the targeted group is already determined by the agency or community group requesting the program. Ideally, the

TABLE 2.7   Step 3: Creating an Intervention Model of Predictive Factors

The following three questions provide the framework for creating an intervention model:

1. Who are the targeted group of young people? What are their ages, grade levels, genders, racial-ethnic groups, socioeconomic levels?

2. What is or are the behavioral objective(s) of the program? Will the program aim to prevent the onset of a behavior? Maintain a health-enhancing behavior? Change a health-compromising behavior? Reduce the occurrence of a behavior? What specifically are the outcomes to be achieved with the targeted group of young people?

3. What factors are predictive of the outcome behavior? Which are most potent? Which are amenable to intervention? What are the key factors that will be the basis of the intervention?

targeted group should be a group in great need of the health behavior program, based on the epidemiologic review and health consequences. The group should be substantial in number, because a community-wide program involves multiple levels of the social environment. The group should be concentrated in a way that a community-wide program will reach them efficiently, particularly through schools. For example, a program aimed at Caucasian females in a multiethnic population will be difficult to implement, because it is unlikely that schools would allow a substantive program for just one ethnic-racial group. However, in a predominantly African American community, a program aimed at African American females would be more acceptable. However, even that definition would likely be too broad. African American 3rd-grade females are obviously different from 10th-grade females; a program will be more successful if it narrows the targeted group to a grade level or developmental stage, such as kindergarten, early elementary, late elementary, middle-junior high school, or high school. In fact, a program for early-elementary-school-age children would be so different from one that is appropriate for high-school-age teens that essentially two health behavior programs would need to be developed. Thus, the targeted group should be representative of the community yet not containing so many major subgroups that separate programs would need to be developed. If multiple subgroups are included, such as multiple racial-ethnic groups, then common factors across groups will need to be considered in program development, as well as including flexibility for cultural differences (Resnicow et al., 1997).

The Outcome Behavior

The outcome behavior should be specific; it is the behavioral objective of the health behavior program. This is quite an important decision to make, because this objective is how the program will be evaluated for its success. Specificity needs to be balanced with the importance of the behavior change and the amount of time and resources available. For example, one objective in CATCH was to reduce fat and sodium in the diet of elementary school children. However, emphasis was given to a healthful diet, and though CATCH promoted eating more fruits and vegetables, whole grains, legumes, and so on, these messages were not as specific as the messages about fat reduction. CATCH achieved changes in dietary fat consumption (Luepker et al., 1996) but not in increased fruit and vegetable consumption (Perry, Lytle, et al., 1998). To increase fruit and vegetable consumption would have required the addition of more specific messages, such as those from the Power Plus study (Perry et al., 1998). Similarly, health behavior programs aimed at smoking prevention alone have, for the most part, been more successful than those that were embedded in drug use prevention efforts (USDHHS, 1994). A notable exception is the Life Skills Training program (Botvin, Baker, Dusenbury, Botvin, & Diaz, 1995). This school-based program has successfully reduced smoking, alcohol, and marijuana use among adolescents; however, the program is quite time intensive over a period of 3 years, allowing ample attention to each of the targeted behaviors.

The behavior selected should be specific about what is expected (the behavioral objective) and for whom (the targeted group). For example, the first phase of Project Northland had as its goal to prevent the onset of alcohol use among young adolescents (Perry, Williams, et al., 1993). The second phase of Project Northland had as its goal to reduce alcohol use among high school students (Komro, Perry, Williams, et al., in press). During Phase I, the intervention focused on resisting influences, learning skills, and providing alternatives to use. During Phase II, emphasis has been on reducing access to alcohol and opportunities to drink. During Phase I, when community members wanted to "do something about drinking at proms," they were redirected to activities more relevant to younger adolescents. (Some newspaper articles were written on the topic of proms, but this did not become a major program component until Phase II.) Thus, the behavioral objective provides the first step in the process of intervention development. Because the outcome behavior is derived from this process of reviewing the literature on health consequences and examining the epidemiologic data, the behavior selected will have a clear rationale that can be communicated to others. The behavioral objective, then, clarifies what is trying to be achieved and for whom and is therefore the goal of the health behavior program to be developed.

Potent Predictive Factors

The final step in creating an intervention model is to identify the predictive factors that are potent and amenable to intervention. Potency refers to the strength of the prediction of each factor. This can be a statistical measure, such as the variance (R^2) in multivariate analyses, which provides a measure of how much of the variation in the behavior is due to the predictive factor. Potency can also be identified by a literature review by how often a given predictive factor is shown to be associated with the behavior, particularly in longitudinal studies where the predictive factor precedes the onset of the behavior. Conrad et al. (1992) reviewed the smoking onset literature in this way. In 27 prospective studies, the number of studies that examined a given predictive factor was identified, and among that subgroup of studies, the number of studies that found the predictive factor to be significantly associated with behavior was calculated. From that review, summarized in the 1994 SGR (USDHHS, 1994, pp. 125, 130), factors such as peer use and approval of cigarettes, behavioral intentions, and opportunities were shown to be predictive of smoking onset in over 80% of the studies. Thus, potency refers to the significance of the association between a predictive factor and the outcome behavior, whether the factor precedes the onset of the behavior, and how many times that association has been replicated. A highly potent factor is able to meet these three criteria: significance, precedence, and replication.

If the literature is scarce on predictive factors for a given behavior, then health behavior theories can guide the selection of factors (Glanz et al., 1997; Nutbeam & Harris, 1998). Hochbaum, Sorenson, and Lorig (1992) provide important suggestions on ways in which theories can successfully be applied by health education practitioners. Still, the more information that is available on what is associated with or precedes a behavior, the more precisely the underlying predictive factors can be identified and targeted by an intervention. The predictive factor should also be amenable to intervention. As mentioned earlier, most of the sociodemographic factors cannot be changed by a community-wide health behavior program, but they can be used in determining the target group. This does not imply that these are not important—inequities need to be addressed in our professional work—but that they are generally beyond the scope of a given program. Other factors that may not be amenable to intervention in a community-wide program include psychological problems (where referral mechanisms can be considered), family dysfunction (which may be outside the public domain), and cultural or societal characteristics (which might require changes in the society at large). Thus, some factors may be more amenable to intervention than others, and this should be considered in selecting the factors to target in a health behavior program.

Creating the Intervention Model

Intervention models were used to develop the health behavior programs discussed in Chapter 1 and were published for the Class of 1989 study (Perry & Jessor, 1985), CATCH (Perry, Stone, et al., 1990), Project Northland (Perry, Williams, et al., 1993), and more generally for adolescent health promotion (Perry, Kelder, et al., 1993). This process of creating models has also been called "intervention mapping" (Cullen, Bartholomew, Parcel, & Kok, 1998). The models each have a basic structure, shown in Figure 2.3.

Thus, to create the intervention model, the predictive factors to be targeted need to be identified. The number of predictive factors should be limited. The reason is that the health behavior program aims to change these predictive factors to change the outcome behavior. To successfully change a predictive and potent factor is exceptionally challenging. Attention, time, and resources need to be allocated in a program to do so. Targeting too many factors generally results in an ineffective program, because each factor did not receive sufficient program attention and thus was not able to be modified. Targeting too few factors also can result in an ineffective

Health Behavior Program

Target Group

Predictive Factors

(Social Environmental, Personal, Behavioral)

Outcome Behavior

Figure 2.3. A Prototype Intervention Model for a Health Behavior Program

program because not enough of the young person's environment, cognitions, or behavior were able to be modified to result in a change in behavior. In statistical terms, we have found that it is most optimal to have a limited number of predictive factors (such as 6 to 8 factors), which together account for 50% or more of the variance in the outcome behavior.

A second guideline in selecting the predictive factors is to include factors from each of the major groups of factors—social environmental, personal, and behavioral. In particular, changes in the social environment have been associated with longer-term changes in behavior (USDHHS, 1994; Wagenaar & Perry, 1994). In addition, factors in the social environment may affect multiple behaviors, so targeting these factors may be both effective and efficient (Perry & Jessor, 1985).

Therefore, from the list of predictive factors identified in Step 2, those factors that are most potent should be starred. Those that are amenable to intervention should also be starred. From the double-starred factors, a limited number should be selected, making sure that social environmental, personal, and behavioral factors are included in the model. This process is shown in Table 2.8, for cigarette smoking onset and young adolescents.

TABLE 2.8 Predictive Factors for Cigarette Smoking Onset and Young Adolescents

Social Environmental Factors

**X	Normative expectations	Most adults and peers smoke cigarettes
**	Normative expectations	Peers think it is OK to smoke
**	Role models	Peers who smoke
	Role models	Parents who smoke
*	Role models	Siblings who smoke
*	Role models	Cigarette advertisements portraying attractive images
**X	Opportunities	Smoking allowed at school
*	Opportunities	Smoking allowed at home
**X	Opportunities	Cigarettes available at vending machines
**	Opportunities	Cigarettes available from small stores
*	Opportunities	Cigarettes not being expensive
**X	Social support	Friends liking to smoke
*	Social support	Parents not supportive

Personal Factors

	Knowledge	Influences to smoke
**X	Knowledge	Ways to resist influences to smoke
*	Values	Friends more important than adults
	Values	Health very important
**X	Functional meanings	Smoking to have fun, be mature, be accepted
*	Self-image	Smoking will enhance my image
**	Self-efficacy	Confidence to refuse peers who want to smoke

Behavioral Factors

**X	Intentions	Expect to smoke in the next year
	Other behaviors	Low academic achievement, alcohol use
**X	Skills	Ability to refuse smoking
	Skills	Ability to engage in healthy activities
*	Incentives	Cigarette industry promotional activities

SOURCE: Conrad et al. (1992), Kelder and Perry (1993), Perry (1998), USDHHS (1994).

* = Potent factor
** = Potent factor and amenable to a community-wide intervention
X = Selected factor for intervention model

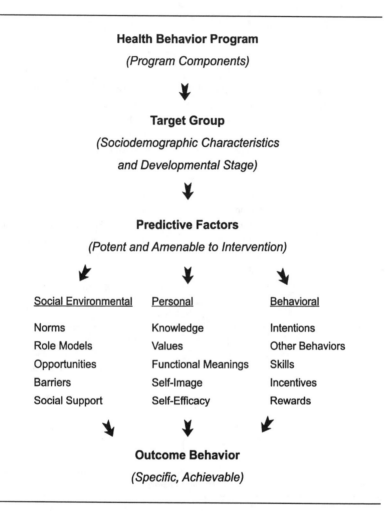

Figure 2.4. A Summary Intervention Model for Health Behavior Change

The last intervention model is shown in Figure 2.4 and can be used as a guide to drive the development of a health behavior program after more information is gathered about the targeted group and the types of program components that may be efficacious. These are discussed in the next chapter.

Therefore, the intervention model specifies the outcome sought, the target group, and the predictive factors that will be the basis of the intervention components. The program developer should be able to succinctly summarize what the health behavior program will accomplish, for whom, and what factors will form the basis of the intervention. This provides the background needed to begin to decide on the program components. For the example of cigarette smoking, a succinct summary would state the following:

> The health behavior program will aim to reduce the onset of cigarette smoking among young adolescents, that is, reduce the percentage of 6th-grade through 8th-grade students who try a cigarette and who experiment with smoking. This will be accomplished by changing the normative expectations that most adults and teens smoke, by reducing opportunities to smoke at school and to obtain cigarettes from vending machines, by creating social support for nonsmoking, by increasing knowledge of ways to resist influences to smoke, by changing the functional meanings of smoking, by reducing intentions to smoke in the future, and by increasing behavioral skills to resist influences to smoke.

This provides clear direction for beginning the types of program components that would be most efficacious.

SUMMARY

This chapter addressed three preliminary steps in the health behavior program development process. These steps are sometimes seen as unnecessary or academic exercises because they require time to review literature and think about the aims of the program and why a behavior persists. Our experience is that these steps are the critical foundation for beginning a community-wide program. They provide the rationale for doing a program, create expertise for the program developer, and use research and theory to design an intervention model that will drive program development. These steps also set the stage for future programs—as the developer learns what works in changing predictive factors, or what is the best "framing" of the health behavior and its consequences, or defends the targeted group selected. Thus, the use of an intervention model begins a cycle that should lead to continued improvements in a health behavior program over time.

3

DETERMINING THE PROGRAM
COMPONENTS

This chapter discusses Steps 4 through 6 in the program development process. It discusses how to write intervention objectives, how to gather information from the targeted group that will be necessary to begin program development, and how to determine what types of program components are most applicable. These steps are necessary precursors to the writing of a program in order to tailor the program for the selected targeted group, to gain knowledge about the various kinds of health behavior programs for children and adolescents concerning a particular behavior, and to avoid "reinventing the wheel" when excellent programs may already be available.

STEP 4: WRITING THE
INTERVENTION OBJECTIVES

In Chapter 2, an intervention model of predictive factors was created, based on theory and the etiologic literature. These factors form the base of the health behavior program as they become intervention objectives. The questions that should be addressed in this step are shown in Table 3.1.

The intervention objectives describe how the predictive factors will be changed by the health behavior program. They can be either positively or negatively related to the outcome behavior, as was illustrated in Perry and Jessor (1985). For example, if "attractive role models who smoke" is the predictive factor, then the intervention objective could be either to reduce the number of attractive role models who smoke or to increase the number of attractive role models who do not smoke. (In the case of antismoking

TABLE 3.1　　Step 4: Writing the Intervention Objectives

The following questions provide the background for deciding on the intervention objectives for a health behavior program:

1. How will the predictive factors be changed by the health behavior program?
2. Can each of the selected predictive factors be written in multiple ways to consider what might be achieved by the health behavior program?
3. Which of the intervention objectives are potentially potent and feasible?

---

campaigns where animals are shown smoking, the intervention objective was to show unappealing or ridiculous role models who do smoke.) If "smoking would make me look cool" is one of the functional meanings of smoking and is a predictor of smoking onset, then the intervention objective could be (a) to make smoking not look cool, (b) to make nonsmoking look cool, or possibly, (c) to make another behavior that is incompatible with smoking look cool.

The intervention objective states how the predictive factor will be changed by the intervention. Each of the selected predictive factors should become one or more intervention objectives. The predictive factors can be viewed in several ways, as shown, and the intervention objectives will reflect this. The intervention objectives, however, are what the program developer will try to achieve through the health behavior program, so careful thought is needed about which intervention objectives will be the most powerful and successful. For example, it may be difficult to reduce the number of role models who smoke, given the difficulty in getting people to quit smoking and young people's high exposure to attractive role models in cigarette advertising on billboards and magazines (Schooler et al., 1996). Therefore, it might be more efficacious to select "increase attractive nonsmoking role models" as an intervention objective, such as through the use of elected peer leaders (Klepp et al., 1986). However, it may be important to include multiple intervention objectives for a given predictive factor, particularly for the most potent predictive factors, so that change in that factor is more likely to be achieved. The program developer should make a list of the intervention objectives from the selected predictive factors that have already been identified.

Table 3.2 provides examples of possible intervention objectives that were derived from the predictive factors of cigarette smoking onset presented in Table 2.8.

TABLE 3.2   Creating Intervention Objectives From the Predictive Factors of Cigarette Smoking Onset

Predictive Factor	Sample Intervention Objectives

Normative expectations
The misperception that most adults and
  peers smoke
	Increase exposure to adults and peers who are
	  nonsmokers
	Decrease exposure to adults and peers
	  who smoke
	Correct misperceptions that most smoke

Opportunities Smoking allowed at school Cigarettes available at vending machines	Do not allow smoking at school Provide healthy activities at school Ban cigarettes in vending machines
Social support Friends who like smoking	Promote having friends who like other activities Promote having friends who do not like smoking Reduce the number of friends who like smoking
Knowledge Ways to resist influences to smoke	Teach ways to be assertive nonsmokers Teach ways to resist influences to smoke

Functional meanings
Smoking to have fun, be mature,
  be accepted
	Portray other activities as fun, mature, and so on
	Portray smoking as not fun, not mature,
	  and so on

Intentions Expect to smoke in the next year	Increase health-enhancing goals Reduce expectations to smoke
Skills Ability to refuse smoking	Practice ways to promote nonsmoking Practice ways to refuse cigarette offers

STEP 5: ENSURING THAT INTERVENTION OBJECTIVES ARE APPLICABLE TO THE TARGETED POPULATION

Understanding how the predictive factors and intervention objectives are perceived by and applicable to the targeted population is critical to the success of a health behavior program. This step provides the opportunity to evaluate how the objectives fit the mind-set of the targeted groups. For example, if the intervention objective is to "increase nonsmoking role models," it is important to know who the influential role models are for the targeted group and how the group perceives smoking role models to

TABLE 3.3   Step 5: Ensuring That Intervention Objectives Are Applicable
to the Targeted Population

The following questions provide the framework for describing how the intervention objectives are perceived by or applicable to the targeted population:

1. Can the intervention objectives be written in language that is understood by the targeted groups? Are the objectives clear and simple?
2. How are intervention objectives applicable to the targeted populations? How are the selected environmental, personal, and behavioral factors evident among young people?
3. How do the targeted groups respond to the intervention objectives? How can changes in these objectives be achieved?

---

develop an effective program for that group. This step takes the program developer, who has become an expert on a health behavior from the data, theory, and literature, to the actual population that will be served. This step also allows the community to become more involved in the intervention design and for the developer to identify people who will support and collaborate in the program, in addition to existing collaborators. The questions that need to be addressed in this step are shown in Table 3.3.

To address these questions, information needs to be gathered from the targeted population.

Intervention Objectives
for the Targeted Group

First, however, the intervention objectives need to be written in a form that is understood by young people and other members of the targeted population. This is critically important—independent of how the information is gathered—because it clarifies what is meant by the intervention objectives in the language of the targeted group and thereby what is going to be accomplished with the health behavior program. In the second phase of Project Northland, based on the outcomes of the Roski et al. (1997) study, we decided to emphasize changing norms around alcohol use in our intervention with high school students (Komro, Perry, Williams, et al., in press). The staff at the university and colleagues in the intervention communities spent considerable time defining what the normative expectations around high school students' alcohol use should be in order to write

TABLE 3.4   Normative Expectations for High School Students' Alcohol
Use: Intervention Objectives From Project Northland

1. Increase the number of people in the community who believe it is unacceptable for high school students to drink.
2. Reduce the number of people who provide alcohol to high school students.
3. Increase the number of adults and high school students who take action when high school students are drinking.
4. Provide opportunities for high school students to have fun, establish their maturity and independence, and relieve stress and boredom without alcohol.
5. Increase parents' understanding of how they can influence their high school students' drinking.
6. Create community events and public places as opportunities for modeling healthy behaviors for high school students.

appropriate intervention objectives that could be shared with community members. The resulting intervention objectives are shown in Table 3.4.

These intervention objectives concerning normative expectations were what we hoped to achieve during the second phase of the project, and how they were perceived by students, parents, young adults, and other community members was important in initiating our interventions.

A second example from Project Northland concerns how functional meanings were defined. The intervention objective was "to increase the importance of reasons not to use alcohol," that is, the functions served by not using alcohol. The negative functional meanings of using alcohol included (a) having better ways to have fun, (b) knowing their parents have rules against alcohol use by people their age, (c) hurting their reputations, (d) fearing that they might become alcoholic, (e) threatening their eligibility to participate in sports, (f) costing too much money, (g) breaking school policies and rules, (h) being bad for their health, (i) hurting their performance as students or athletes, and (j) wanting to make their own decisions and not give in to peer pressure. Several of these functional meanings became intervention objectives and were incorporated into the Project Northland programs. For example, our sixth-grade program encouraged parents to have explicit rules with consequences concerning alcohol use for their young adolescent child (Williams et al., 1995). Our surveys provided information on which were the most important reasons, and

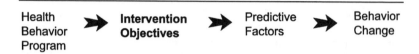

Figure 3.1.

nearly all of these reasons were significantly changed during the first phase of the project (Perry et al., 1996).

Thus, during this step, the intervention objectives should be defined based on the literature and the identified predictive factors but written so that they are understandable to young people, parents, and other community members. The intervention objectives clarify even more precisely what is to be achieved by the intervention, and it is important to be able to communicate those in clear, simple language. Figure 3.1 provides the general model described.

Information on the Intervention Objectives From the Targeted Groups

Information concerning the intervention objectives can be obtained from the targeted groups in several ways, including (a) existing data and reports, (b) surveys of a representative sample of the targeted population, (c) structured interviews, (d) observations, and (e) focus groups. The purpose of obtaining information is to verify that the predictive factors and intervention objectives are appropriate for the targeted group, how the factors and intervention objectives are perceived, and ways in which they might be approached in a health behavior program. Again, when there are just a limited number of predictive factors, finding out how the targeted groups perceive these factors becomes more feasible. This step is particularly critical when there is limited experience with, and therefore a limited literature on, a particular behavior or population (Gittelsohn et al., 1998). This step could also be considered a needs assessment of the intervention objectives, because it helps to clarify "what is" versus "what should be," from the perspective of the targeted population (Witkin & Altschuld, 1995). This process allows considerable opportunity to identify those who can support or collaborate in the development or implementation of the program.

Existing Data

Data or reports may already exist concerning the behavior of the targeted group and one or more of the predictive factors. This is particularly the case for larger urban areas, communities near universities, or groups that have been previously studied. It is important in this step, however, that the data come from the targeted group rather than from national data sources.

For example, the second phase of Project Northland was guided, in part, by the data and experiences of the first phase. Annual surveys had been done with adolescents in the Project Northland communities, which included data on their behavior and other predictive factors of alcohol use. The first phase of Project Northland had been successful in reducing young adolescent alcohol use by 8th grade (Perry et al., 1996). This was attributable to changes in peer influence, parent-child communications, functional meanings, and self-efficacy. No significant changes were observed in the outer ring of the social environment, particularly with young people's perceived or actual ability to get alcohol. Thus, the second phase focused on reducing access to alcohol from commercial and social sources, because access to alcohol was seen as a significant predictor in adolescent alcohol use (Wagenaar & Perry, 1994). Our surveys revealed that very few parents or community leaders thought that it was OK for high school students to drink, yet over one third of high school students and young adults aged 18 to 22 thought it was acceptable. This was particularly troubling because social sources of alcohol, from peers and older adolescents, were the primary ways in which high school students obtained alcohol. Thus, our intervention objectives around changing normative expectations (shown in Table 3.4)—that it is unacceptable for high school students to drink and unacceptable to provide alcohol to high school students—were a result of information from the high school students themselves. We felt the project needed to be very clear and firm about not providing alcohol to high school students and not approving of drinking at that age.

Survey Data

New data can be obtained from the targeted group through surveys, interviews, observations, and focus groups. Each of these has advantages and disadvantages. Written surveys can generally provide data from more people than can interviews or focus groups, because the latter are personal and time intensive with the participants. Also, in surveys, the same set of questions can be asked of all respondents, so the range and consistency of responses can be analyzed. With a representative sample of the targeted group, surveys can provide valid and reliable data on which to base intervention development. However, conducting a written quantitative survey is a project in itself, has its own set of scientific rules of acceptability, generally requires time for data entry and analyses, and can therefore be expensive to undertake (Creswell, 1994). Unless there is a mechanism in place to collect data from the targeted group (such as a preintervention survey), community surveys are usually outside the scope of an intervention developer. Smaller surveys in conjunction with interviews, observations, and focus groups may be more efficient and useful. A thorough discussion on designing surveys can be found in Creswell (1994).

In-Depth Interviews

Interviews are particularly useful in obtaining information from people on how they understand their world (Kvale, 1996). They allow the program developer to search for reactions and perceptions about the intervention objectives but using the mode of a normal conversation and without the influence of other observers. In Project Northland, face-to-face semistructured interviews were conducted by staff with community members at the beginning of the second phase of the project. The purpose of the interviews was to explain the goals of the second phase, get reactions to the intervention objectives, and explore the types of self-interest community members had in adolescent alcohol use. About 100 one-on-one interviews were conducted in each community—a lengthy and time-consuming process. However, the interviews provided the program developers with considerable information about each community, particularly concerning the people who could powerfully affect the goals of the project and the power structure of the community, from many people's perspectives. Without other people present, community members were more willing to share their reactions to the goals of the project, the norms that were trying to be changed, and their own personal experiences concerning alcohol use and abuse. From the interviews, key people were selected to serve on community action teams, and the intervention objectives at the community level were able to be tailored to the needs of each community. Greater detail on how to conduct interviews can be found in Kvale (1996).

Observations

Systematic observations of the targeted group or community can also be undertaken to assess the appropriateness of the intervention objectives (Witkin & Altschuld, 1995). These can be unobtrusive measures in that the targeted group is often unaware they are being monitored. Observations can be particularly useful in assessing the appropriateness of environmental and behavioral factors, because they can often be observed. For example, in Project Northland, alcohol purchase attempt observational studies were conducted by young-looking 21-year-old females in all of the alcohol outlets in our intervention communities (Forster et al., 1994). These females were judged by a panel to appear to be 18 years old or younger. The females attempted to buy six-packs of beer without showing their identification. We found that these young women were able to purchase beer half of the time without being asked for identification and in 80% of the outlets (because each outlet was visited multiple times). These data clearly demonstrated the need for our intervention objective of reducing commercial access to alcohol for high school students.

A second example, from the Power Plus study, was the systematic observation of children at lunch. Children were observed in the lunch line, and the foods selected were recorded; they were then observed while eating to record any food that was shared. Last, their lunch trays were observed when they had finished eating to note any leftover food. From these observations, a quantitative record of what the child had eaten was obtained (Perry, Bishop et al., 1998). It was observed that the children ate more fruits and vegetables when a greater variety was offered in the lunch line and when the Power Plus program was ongoing in the classroom.

Focus Groups

A focus group is defined as a "carefully planned discussion designed to obtain perceptions of a defined area of interest in a permissive, nonthreatening environment" (Krueger, 1988, p. 18). As such, focus groups are ideal for assessing the appropriateness of intervention objectives, because they are a defined area of inquiry, and honest perceptions are being sought. Focus groups have been used extensively in the development of advertising and marketing of commercial products, because they are seen as a way to obtain information from a targeted group at a reasonable cost (Krueger, 1988). Focus groups, rather than making recommendations or building consensus on an issue, provide a mechanism for obtaining the perceptions of the targeted group on ideas, programs, or products. They may also be used with groups other than the targeted group, such as teachers, parents, and community members, to provide additional information and insight on the intervention objectives.

Focus groups generally consist of 7 to 10 individuals, who may or may not know each other yet are selected to be alike based on the purpose of the groups. For example, when exploring whether and how young adults provide alcohol to high school students, focus groups with 18-year-olds to 22-year-olds were conducted. Information obtained from these focus groups were consistent with what we had found in the Project Northland surveys, that 18-year-olds to 22-year-olds did provide alcohol. But the focus groups also allowed us to explore several additional questions, such as why they provided, how and where it was done, and what would be effective in changing these practices. It was important that we learned about their perceptions to these questions in their own language. The groups mentioned that they sometimes felt guilty providing alcohol, particularly worrying that something might happen to the high school student. They were unaware of the legal consequences of being caught providing alcohol. They responded to a theme that adults (as 18-year-olds to 22-year-olds perceive themselves) are old enough to act responsibly and not provide to kids. From those insights, a "Don't Provide" campaign was developed that was specifically aimed at 18-year-olds to 22-year-olds and that was based on the reasons and methods revealed in the focus groups. It had the subtheme, "They're just kids, for crying out loud!" This information would not have been possible to gather from interviews, surveys, or observations, because the focus group leaders could not anticipate the responses and were able to probe in new areas.

Because the focus group discussions are like social discussions, they are generally enjoyable and interesting to the participants, and they allow for interactions to occur among participants, and new information is revealed in the process. Thus, focus groups have the advantages of flexibility, quick feedback, and not being too expensive. They require trained or skilled leaders, multiple groups to ensure reliable perceptions, the ability to organize and schedule groups, and an environment conducive to an open

TABLE 3.5   Information-Gathering Methods From the Targeted Groups

Method	Advantages	Disadvantages
1. Existing survey data	Savings in time and money Potentially longitudinal data Potentially reliable & valid tools	May not be the targeted group Questions may not be as relevant as possible
2. New survey data	Representative sample Large sample possible Potentially reliable & valid tools	Requires time and money Questions may be limited in scope
3. In-depth interviews	Selected sample Can be open-ended Can be more personal	Usually limited to smaller sample
4. Direct observation	Selected sample Can be unobtrusive Limits reporting bias	Assesses environment and behavior only Perceptions limited
5. Focus groups	Not expensive Open-ended discussion Quick results Community involvement	Difficult to recruit sample Special training needed Difficult to schedule

discussion (Krueger, 1988). A excellent guide for conducting focus groups is *The Focus Group Kit* (Morgan & Krueger, 1998).

An outgrowth of focus groups has been the formation of community advisory groups to provide feedback on intervention objectives. These are ongoing focus groups that are organized during the development of the health behavior program and may continue during implementation. The members of these groups represent the targeted group, advise the program developers, and ensure that the intervention objectives are tailored to their community. The members also serve as liaisons to the community and, as such, facilitate the acceptance and implementation of the completed program.

The advantages of and drawbacks to each of the types of information-gathering methods just discussed are shown in Table 3.5. Based on the circumstances and skills of the program developer and characteristics of the community and the targeted groups, one or more of these methods may be used to assess whether the intervention objectives are appropriate, how they are perceived by the targeted group, and how they might be approached in a health behavior program.

As a result of Step 5, the program developer should have a much better understanding of the targeted groups in the community and how the members of these groups perceive the intervention objectives. A summary of the data or information that is obtained should be written by listing the intervention objectives for each of the selected factors. Then, there should be information on each objective that has been obtained from the targeted groups. From the example given earlier for Project Northland, the predictive factor was the norm that it was OK to provide alcohol to high school students. The intervention objective was to "reduce the number of people who provide alcohol to high school students." From existing data from Project Northland, we found that 18-year-olds to 22-year-olds were most likely to provide alcohol to high school students. From focus groups with this age group, we found why they provided alcohol (returning the "favor" from their high school years), how this occurred (primarily at parties), and what might get them not to provide (the reality that someone might get harmed; that it wasn't how an "adult" would behave). These became the background information that was needed to create the health behavior program, a process that will be discussed in the next chapter. Similarly, information has been gathered from junior high and high school students, teachers, parents, community leaders, police, merchants, food service personnel, coaches, etc., to guide the development of health behavior programs, using one or more of the methods recently discussed. This information has been invaluable in ensuring that the program meets the needs of a given community and will be relevant to the targeted groups.

STEP 6: DETERMINING WHICH TYPES OF PROGRAMS ARE MOST APPLICABLE

Health behavior programs for children and adolescents take place within their social environments, such as in their homes, schools, and communities (Poland, Rootman, & Green, in press). The program developer will need to review the types of programs that have previously taken place concerning the selected health behavior, carefully examine those programs that have demonstrated behavior change with the targeted population, and

TABLE 3.6   Step 6: Determining Which Types of Programs Are Most Applicable

The following three questions provide the framework for selecting the types of programs to be developed for the health behavior program:

1. What are the primary types of programs? What are the advantages and disadvantages of these programs?
2. What programs have previously been developed concerning the selected health behavior? Have any programs had positive outcomes? What were the key components of those programs? Which predictive factors were changed?
3. Which types of programs will be most potent and be able to reach the greatest percentage of the targeted groups? Which programs will be most likely to meet the intervention objectives?

consider the practical aspects of each type of program. Decisions about which types of programs to implement will be based on an understanding of the potential and past successes of each type of program. Questions to guide Step 6 are shown in Table 3.6.

Types of Health Behavior Programs

The primary types of health behavior programs for children and adolescents are those that (a) occur in schools, (b) involve parents, (c) organize peer groups, (d) create environmental change, or (e) mobilize communities to take action—or some combination of these. There are other potential sites for health behavior programs, such as at churches, through health care organizations, within community organizations and clubs, and even on the Internet. The research base for these sites has not been as extensive as for the types selected; still, these may be very promising and applicable to a particular behavior or targeted group. The discussions in this section should be relevant to health behavior programs in those additional settings as well.

In this section, each of these five types of programs will be reviewed. Each type of program has advantages and disadvantages, a record of success in the research literature, and existing resources that are available for the program developer. Each type of program has potential costs associated with it, and these costs need to be assessed and balanced against the potency of the program. A program is potent when it successfully meets an intervention objective, changes a predictive factor, and can do so with a large number of young people. Thus, an effective health behavior program is both potent and pervasive—able to create change across the entire community.

School-Based Programs

Schools are a logical site for health behavior programs, because young people spend considerable time in school. Programs at school have the potential to reach a large percentage of children and adolescents over multiple years, because over 95% of those aged 5 to 17 are enrolled in school (Kann et al., 1995). Schools are often the hubs of their communities, with outreach to parents and community members (Dryfoos, 1994). In addition, the goals of schooling are consistent with the goals of healthier behavior—to enable young people to be able to assume roles of partners, providers, parents, and citizens as adults (Kann et al., 1995). The importance of school health behavior programs has been recognized in several government documents, including *Healthy People 2000*, where Objective 8.4 states that three fourths of the schools in the United States should have planned and coordinated school health programs from kindergarten through 12th grade (Collins et al., 1995). However, there are also challenges to implementing programs in schools. Program developers must work within the time constraints of the school program and generally must seek approval for program content from parents, teachers, administrators, and school boards. As schools become more focused on basic skills development, graduation standards, and achievement tests and as more demands are placed on schools to remedy a variety of youth behavior problems, each program will be scrutinized to ensure that it is crucial, potent, efficient, and appropriate for *their* schools. Another disadvantage of working with schools is that although the peer group is often formed in schools, alienated higher-risk students may have dropped out by high school or may not be as receptive in the school setting as they might be in other settings.

A variety of programs have been undertaken at schools to improve the health behavior of young people (Allensworth & Kolbe, 1987; Resnicow & Allensworth, 1996). Table 3.7 lists the primary types of health behavior programs for children and adolescents, including some of the characteristics of successful programs.

TABLE 3.7 Types of School-Based Health Behavior Programs for Young People

Classroom curricula	Lessons in the classroom taught or facilitated by teachers, peer leaders, nurses, health educators, or other experts. Successful programs have had multiple sessions, were interactive, experiential, developmentally appropriate, and aimed at skill development.
Homework	Assignments from classroom teachers to be carried out at home. Programs have required parental involvement, been experiential, aimed at skill development, and included incentives for program completion.
Physical education	Classes on physical education taught by teachers and coaches. Programs have emphasized moderate-to-vigorous activities with active participation.
Food service	Changes in the food served in the school meals program. This has included lower-fat and lower-sodium recipes and vendor products, as well as increasing the number of choices of each of the school meal components.
Extracurricular	Programs outside of the classroom. These have occurred at breaks, at lunch, or after school hours. They have included activities structured by the schools, such as after-school activities and sports, or other opportunities, such as school-based health clinics, health services, or peer action groups.
School policies	Policies and rules concerning young people's behavior. These have included whether the school was smoke free, how alcohol use was handled, the types and cost of foods that were available in vending machines and snack lines, or the ways conflicts were mediated.

The program developer should begin by doing a review of existing school-based programs for the particular health behavior. Excellent resources to begin this review include the *Handbook of Adolescent High Risk Behavior* (DiClemente, Hansen, & Ponton, 1996), *Healthy Children 2010* (Weissberg, Gullotta, Adams, Hampton, & Ryan, 1997), and the Division of Adolescent and School Health at the Centers for Disease Control and Prevention (http://www.cdc.gov/nccdphp/dash). The latter agency has, over the past decade, developed guidelines for school health programs in the areas of physical activity (CDC, 1997), healthy eating (CDC, 1996a), tobacco use (CDC, 1994), and AIDS prevention (CDC, 1988). These guidelines are the result of a consensus of the research literature and experts, provide excellent direction for future programs, and include references to successful programs in these behavioral areas.

In addition, informative reviews have been undertaken on the state of school health policies and programs (Kann et al., 1995), school-based health clinics (Dryfoos, 1994, 1998), after-school programs (Carnegie Council on Adolescent Development, 1992), school food service research (Lytle, Kelder, & Snyder, 1992), substance use prevention curricula (Drug Strategies, 1996; Dusenbury & Falco, 1995; Hansen, 1992; Pentz et al., 1989), violence prevention strategies for schools (Drug Strategies, 1998), smoking prevention (USDHHS, 1994), nutrition education (Contento et al., 1995) and physical activity programs (CDC, 1997). Innovative school-based programs for specific populations should also be reviewed (Caballero et al., in press). The promotion of full-service schools, to accommodate a range of young people's health and social concerns, is cogently described in *Safe Passage* (Dryfoos, 1998) and provides an optimal view of what can be accomplished in schools.

All of the research programs described in Chapter 1 included behavioral classroom curricula. These curricula were potent because they allowed intensive behavioral instruction to occur over several hours of classroom time, such as self-monitoring of fruit and vegetable servings in Power Plus, practicing refusal skills in Project Northland and the Class of 1989 Study, goal setting to change types of snacks in CATCH, and modeling of peer leaders in the WHO Study. Homework was included in the Class of 1989 Study, CATCH, and Project Northland. These were extensions of the curricula as well as parental involvement programs, soon to be discussed. The Class of 1989 Study and CATCH sought changes in physical activity levels of youths. In the Class of 1989 Study, the physical education classes were the site of a community-wide activity contest, but only changes in physical activity outside of class were sought (Klepp, Perry, & Hawkins, 1985). In CATCH, changes in physical education classes resulted in greater time spent in moderate-to-vigorous activities during class and more vigorous activity among children. Both CATCH and Power Plus sought and achieved changes in food service offerings, with CATCH emphasizing reductions in the percentage of calories from fat in school lunch and Power Plus seeking to increase fruit and vegetable consumption. CATCH and Project Northland both worked with school administrators to change policies and practices around cigarette smoking and alcohol use, respectively.

The school-based programs in these studies emphasized changes in environmental (norms, opportunities, support, role models), behavioral (skills, intentions, incentives), and personal factors (behavioral capability, functional meanings, self-efficacy), which in turn were effective in creating change in the targeted behaviors. Thus, all five projects included school-based programs as a key component of the interventions; the school-based programs were largely responsible for the outcomes observed from these studies. Because the school-based components were so extensive in these projects, greater detail on activities within particular programs can be found in the cited publications.

Parental Involvement Programs

The importance of parents in influencing their children's health behaviors has been a topic of common interest and research for decades (Morgaine, 1992). Parents are generally the most powerful role models for their children, provide substantial opportunities for and barriers to their behavior, and are those most concerned for their children's health and well-being (Baranowski & Nader, 1985; Johnson et al., 1994; Kledges et al., 1983). Parental involvement programs, when successful, can have a potent impact on their children (Nader et al., 1992; Perry et al., 1988; Williams & Perry, 1998; Williams et al., 1995; Williams et al., 1999). However, parents are difficult to reach in large numbers with an intensive program. Health education classes for parents do not usually attract a large audience (Perry, 1986). U.S. parents have busy schedules so that health behavior programs need to fit within these lifestyles. There are increasingly various family structures that also need to be accommodated in health behavior programs (Perry et al., 1993). In some cases, parents' own behavior may contribute to a problem around a given health behavior (Kinston, Loader, & Miller, 1988; Nader et al., 1989), and those parents may not be receptive to a given program. Homes are the private domains of individuals and families, so any health behavior program that is implemented in homes will need to be voluntary and provide tangible benefits to parents.

A variety of parental involvement programs have been implemented to improve the health behavior of young people. Table 3.8 lists these types of programs, including some of the characteristics of successful programs.

Resources for the program developer include programs in the research literature that can be identified through a literature search, such as the San

TABLE 3.8 Types of Parent Involvement Programs

Home teams	Homework assigned in school requiring parent or family involvement. Successful programs have been user-friendly, creative and attractive, had multiple sessions, were interactive, were culturally and developmentally appropriate, aimed at skill development, and included incentives for program completion.
Family fun nights	Evening, after-school, or weekend educational sessions with information, food, activities, and games. Programs have used games and activity stations rather than lectures, were experiential and entertaining, and aimed at skill development.
Direct mail	Information sent directly to the parents. Programs have used video- and audiotapes, booklets, postcards, calendars, and contests.
Home visits	Educational sessions with parents at their homes given by a health educator, nurse, nutritionist, and so forth. Programs have focused on personalized problem solving and skill development.
Parent organizations	Parent groups that meet to mobilize other parents and community members. Parents have also been recruited as members of community groups. Successful groups have had focused activities, training, and self-interest of members in the identified problem.

Diego Family Health Project (Nader et al., 1989; Patterson et al., 1988), the Family Health Project (Nader et al., 1983), the Hearty Heart Home Team (Perry et al., 1988), obesity prevention programs (Epstein & Wing, 1987), high-risk adolescents in the Adolescent Transitions Program (Andrews, Soberman, & Dishion, 1995; Dishion & Andrews, 1995), and general parenting practices (Morgaine, 1992). Other program resources are available through the U.S. Department of Agriculture, which sponsors the Children, Youth and Families Education and Research Network and the National Network for Family Resiliency. Their web sites are, respectively, http://www.cyfernet.mes.umn.edu and http://www.nnfr.org/nnfr.

In the programs described in Chapter 1, CATCH, Power Plus, and Project Northland had home team programs to accompany the classroom curricula. CATCH included homework materials to accompany the curricula. Power Plus provided "snack packs," which included the ingredients for healthy snacks for the whole family. However, only the home team program for Project Northland, the Slick Tracy Program for sixth graders, demonstrated impact on predictive factors (Perry et al., 1996; Williams et al., 1995). The lack of effect of the home team programs in CATCH was surprising, because the third-grade program, the Hearty Heart Home Team, had been more powerful than the corresponding classroom program in a prior study (Perry et al., 1988) and had been successful in reducing the percentage of calories of fat in children's diets. The original home team program employed college students and university staff as "coaches" and a grand prize to increase participation (which were not feasible in CATCH), suggesting that attractive role models and incentives may be necessary if changes in behavior are to be achieved.

CATCH and Project Northland also organized fun nights for families. These events were attended by over 50% of the parents (Perry et al., 1997; Williams et al., 1995). This high participation rate was most likely due to the "fun" nature of the evening (they were not advertised as educational events), with food being served and because the students (their children) were actively involved in the evening by either performing or presenting projects. Previous work with parent evenings over a 1-year time period showed a significant impact on children's heart health (Nader et al., 1989), suggesting that parent education can be effective if it can maintain participation over a long time period. Project Northland sent direct mail to the parents, including parent-child communication programs, parenting tips called "Northland Notes for Parents," calendars, postcards, and interactive contests. Participation rates were considerably lower for direct mail programs than for the home teams, perhaps because the latter required adult participation as part of the school curriculum. None of the projects attempted home visits as part of a health behavior program due to the high costs, even though this has shown to be successful in other studies (Tell, 1982). Project Northland actively recruited parents to be part of the community task forces that addressed changes in the larger community. This strategy has been more actively pursued during the second phase of the project. The family involvement programs in these research studies aimed at changes in environmental (opportunities, role models, support, norms), behavioral (trial behavior, skills, incentives) and personal factors (values, knowledge). Thus, three of the five projects had active parental involvement programs, although all were linked to the school-based program.

Peer Involvement

Peer influence has been labeled among the most influential factors in determining young people's behavior (Hansen et al., 1987; Klepp et al. 1986; USDHHS, 1994). Peers act as role models of new behaviors and their consequences (Bandura, 1977). They help to create the norms concerning behavior, particularly whether or not the behavior is acceptable to the peer group (Hansen & Graham, 1991). The peer group creates social opportunities in which health behaviors are carried out, such as snacking with friends, drinking at parties, or playing sports. To increasingly value peers and the peer group is normal during adolescence in U.S. society (Crockett & Petersen, 1993; Perry et al., 1993), although the influence of peers is generally characterized as negative. Peer involvement in health behavior programs, then, particularly during early adolescence, may be critical to their success (Black et al., 1998), because potent peer influences can be channeled to promote healthier behaviors (Komro et al., 1996; Perry, Klepp, Halper, Hawkins, & Murray, 1986). Peer involvement programs have the disadvantage of being outside the usual school curriculum and programs and so require either additional commitment of time and resources by a school or an outside agency to support them. Because young people, like their parents, have busy schedules, recruiting them to be involved is also more difficult because of the time required outside of class.

There are several types of peer involvement programs that have been evaluated in health behavior programs. These are described in Table 3.9.

Resources for effective peer involvement programs include those found in the literature on peer leadership (Bell, Ellickson, & Harrison, 1993; Black et al., 1998; Botvin, Baker, Renick, Filazzola, & Botvin, 1984), peer counseling and mediation (Drug Strategies, 1998; Henriksen, 1991; Johnson, Johnson, & Dudley, 1992; Kim, McLeod, Rader, & Johnston, 1992; Komro, Perry, Veblen-Mortenson, et al., in press; Resnik & Gibbs, 1981; Robinson, Morrow, Kigin, & Lindemann, 1991; Switzer, Simmons, Dew, Regalski, & Wang, 1995), and peer participation programs (Komro, Perry, Veblen-Mortenson, & Williams, 1994). Additional programs for peer involvement can be found through the National Peer Helpers Association (1990), which has specific standards for peer involvement; Students Against Drunk Driving, a youth advocacy group; and the peer program

TABLE 3.9   Types of Peer Involvement Programs

Peer leadership programs	Peers are elected by classmates to lead prevention programs. Successful programs include extensive training, concrete activities, rehearsal, an adult coordinator, and reinforcements.
Peer counseling and mediation	Peers help others who have social and behavioral problems. Include extensive training as a separate course in school and an adult counselor for ongoing supervision.
Peer participation and action	Peers volunteer to create, plan, and implement programs in their schools or communities concerning a particular goal. Include skills training, advocacy training, funding, and adult involvement.

resources that are available on the Internet (http://www.islandnet. com/rcarr/helping.html).

Peer involvement has been a primary component in my research with adolescents, because it empowers young people to take charge of their social environment and to create healthier norms and values for their generation. Because many of the behaviors of concern, such as eating, tobacco and alcohol use, are social behaviors to adolescents, peer involvement in the process of change seems critical. In the WHO Study, an alcohol education program taught by selected or volunteer peers was compared with the same program taught by teachers and a no-program control (Perry, Grant et al., 1989). This was done in four very different countries (Australia, Chile, Norway, Swaziland) on four continents. In all the countries, the peer-led program resulted in lower alcohol use than in the other two conditions. Thus, in this study, peer leaders clearly were the critical component of the intervention.

In the Class of 1989 Study, peer leadership was part of each of the school curricula from the 6th through 10th grades. Peer leaders, elected because they were "liked and respected" by their classmates, were trained each year to conduct the programs in the classrooms. These included smoking, alcohol, and drug use prevention programs and healthy eating and physical activity curricula. Peer leaders were most effective in the junior high school years, seventh through ninth grades, and benefited even more from the programs than did their classmates (Klepp et al., 1994).

Because Project Northland was a community-wide intervention study during middle school and high school, multiple types of peer involvement programs were implemented and evaluated. Peer leaders were elected, trained by local field staff, and facilitated the sixth-grade and seventh-grade classroom curricula (Komro, Perry, Veblen-Mortenson, et al., in press; Perry et al., 1996). Students volunteered in the seventh and eighth grades to form groups to plan alcohol-free social activities for their peers. These peer participation groups were facilitated by adult volunteers and resulted in lower alcohol use among those who were active planners (Komro et al., 1996). During the high school years, 11th-grade and 12th-grade students volunteered to be members of peer action teams. These teams worked outside of school with a local adult coordinator on projects that would affect alcohol availability and use by high school students. These experiences with peer involvement have generally required additional personnel and specially written curricula. However, the costs have been far outweighed by what the teens learned from being leaders and from the impact that they had on their peers (Black et al., 1998).

Environmental Change

Creating a healthy physical environment is seen as one of the five major areas for health promotion activities as defined by the Ottawa Charter for Health Promotion (WHO, 1986). Environmental changes are consistent with a public health approach to prevention, where the community as a whole becomes responsible for the health and well-being of its citizens (Forster, 1982). Creating changes in the physical environments of young people may be critical to sustaining changes that have been made in the schools, at home, or with the peer group. If opportunities exist throughout the physical environment, then young people are more likely to engage in healthier behaviors. Similarly, if barriers to unhealthy behavior exist throughout the community, young people are less likely to engage in these behaviors. Environmental changes help make the enactment of healthier behavior "passive" and do not rely as much on individual choice (Forster, 1982).

An example of the potency of the physical environment is cigarette advertising. Cigarette advertising is 3 times more influential with adolescents than it is with adults (Pollay et al., 1996). If nonsmoking adolescents can identify a favorite cigarette advertisement, then they are significantly more likely to make the transition to smoking than those who do not have a favorite advertisement (Pierce et al., 1998). Moreover, during the period of the Fairness Doctrine, 1967 to 1971, when antismoking advertisements were mandated, with about 1 antismoking message to every 12 prosmoking advertisements, adolescent smoking declined, suggesting that counteradvertisements with sufficient frequency can counter cigarette advertising (Perry, 1998; Pierce & Gilpin, 1995; USDHHS, 1994). The passive exposure to messages about cigarettes in the environment, through advertising and promotional activities, plays a significant role in the onset of smoking (Perry, 1998).

Thus, for a given behavior, the program developer might examine whether a behavior is possible (when, where, and how?) and whether it is positively or negatively promoted (where and how?). These will provide cues as to the types of environmental changes that might be targeted in a health behavior program. Changes in the physical environment become permanent changes in the opportunity structure of a community. However, achieving these changes often requires community organizing and political action and can be time-consuming and expensive to implement. Some examples of environmental change programs are shown in Table 3.10.

Resources for environmental change programs are less abundant than school, family, and peer programs, in part because they are generally large-scale efforts that have been more difficult to evaluate using community trials methodologies. This may reflect the orientation in the United States to prefer programs that emphasize individual responsibility (Forster, 1982). Also, environmental change programs are often a result of policy changes, which will be discussed next. Still, excellent case studies and reviews are available on the topics mentioned, and more outcome research is forthcoming (see CDC, 1997; Fitzpatrick, Chapman, & Barr, 1997; Flores, 1995; Food Marketing Institute, 1987; Glanz et al., 1995; Nichols & Schmidt, 1995; Ozer et al., 1997; Phillips & Bradshaw, 1993; Sallis, 1993; Sellers, McGraw, & McKinlay, 1994; Smith, Weinman, & Parrilli, 1997; Trussell, Koenig, Steward, & Darroch, 1997; USDHHS, 1994; Wagenaar & Perry, 1994).

Among the health behavior programs discussed in Chapter 1, the Class of 1989 Study and Project Northland included environmental change strategies. The Class of 1989 Study was embedded in the larger Minnesota

TABLE 3.10   Examples of Environmental Change Programs

Healthy eating	Restaurant menus with lower-fat, lower-calorie items Grocery stores with labels for healthier choices 5-A-Day mass media programs
Physical activity	Exercise courses in parks Bike lanes and walking paths Having gyms and recreation areas open and available
Smoking	Removing cigarette vending machines Counteradvertising campaigns Removing billboard and point-of-purchase advertising Promoting smoke-free establishments
Alcohol use	Alcohol-free social clubs for teens (i.e., coffee houses) Fewer alcohol outlets Restrictions at community events (i.e., roped-off areas)
Teenage pregnancy	Condom availability School health clinics

Heart Health Program. The Minnesota Heart Health Program promoted environmental changes, such as restaurant and grocery store labeling and increased opportunities to engage in physical activity. Mass media promoted healthier eating and physical activity patterns, nonsmoking, and blood pressure surveillance and compliance with blood pressure medication (Mittelmark et al., 1986). The outcomes of the Class of 1989 Study were sustained following the classroom behavioral curricula, and these long-term outcomes were attributed to the reinforcement of the curricula by the community changes of the larger Minnesota Heart Health Program (Perry et al., 1994a). The larger social and physical environments changed to be consistent with what was being taught in the schools. In Project Northland, community and peer action teams worked on projects that would lead to community-wide change in adolescent alcohol use. Some of these projects included alternative activities, alcohol-free recreational facilities, mass media campaigns, and point-of-purchase media (Komro et al., 1994; Komro, Perry, Williams, et al., in press). Thus, the two projects that involved community-level changes sought change in the community environment to support healthier behavior. Still, more effort to change the environment is warranted, given its direct effect on behavior, and should be seriously considered by program developers.

Community Organizing and Action

Changes in communities, in their policies and practices and priorities, are necessary to create and sustain healthy behaviors among youth (Breslow, 1990; Forster, 1982; Nutbeam, 1997). In the Ottawa Charter, building healthful public policy and strengthening community action were two of the five major action areas for health promotion:

Health promotion works through concrete and effective community action in setting priorities, making decisions, planning strategies, and implementing them to achieve better health. At the heart of this process is the empowerment of communities, their ownership and control of their own endeavors and destinies. (WHO, 1986, p. 1)

Community action is achieved through a variety of methods, including advocacy, community task forces and coalitions, and direct action strategies. All of these methods seek change at the level of the community— specifically, the outer ring of the social environment—and so are able, in turn, to affect change throughout the other levels. Thus, the purview of community action is the community as a whole, including laws, policies, resources, and activities that affect the entire population. The advantages of this approach are that the changes become part of the normative expectations of a community, become systematized within the community bureaucracy, and support changes made in schools, homes, workplaces, and so forth. The disadvantages of this approach are that changes are inherently part of a political process, often require consensus of a large number of people, take considerable time to achieve, and can be overturned (such as after an election). Descriptions of the types of community action approaches are shown in Table 3.11.

There are excellent resources for community action efforts, including *Health Promotion at the Community Level* (Bracht, 1990, 1999), which describes community organizing principles and approaches, and Part 4 of *Health Behavior and Health Education* (Glanz et al., 1997), which describes the history and key components of exemplary community-level change approaches. An excellent description of direct action community

TABLE 3.11 Community Action Approaches

Advocacy strategies	Groups in the community define, identify, and frame a problem and stimulate media coverage, public concern, and action.
Community organizing	Collaboration and the use of consensus, cooperation, and capacity-building among community members so that communities can identify problems and their solutions.
Direct action strategies	Efforts within communities where conflicting values exist and these differences are used to mobilize individuals to action by holding leaders accountable for decisions affecting the community.

organizing, the process that was used in the Tobacco Policy Options Program, can be found in Blaine et al. (1997) and Forster et al. (1998). This studies demonstrate that teenage smoking rates can be reduced through the application of direct action strategies alone. Media advocacy approaches are described in *Media Advocacy and Public Health: Power for Prevention* (Wallack, Dorfman, Jernigan, & Themba, 1993). Issues around empowerment approaches are discussed in *Studies of Empowerment* (Rappaport, Swift, & Hess, 1984).

Project Northland used all three types of community action approaches during Phases I and II. During Phase I, community task forces were formed in each of the 14 intervention communities, facilitated by Project Northland staff member who resided in the community. The task forces selected numerous activities to implement to prevent young-adolescent alcohol use, including educational programs, alternative activities for teens, and a gold card program where young people could obtain discounts from businesses by remaining drug free. However, these activities did not result in any measurable changes in young people's access to alcohol (Perry et al., 1996). During Phase II, based on prior work with tobacco (Forster et al., 1998), direct action strategies were supported in each community, led by an organizer from the local community. These strategies sought changes in the policies and practices within these communities to reduce teenage access to alcohol. Within these efforts, a media advocacy campaign was introduced, the *Don't Provide* campaign. Each community decided whether and how to build on this campaign. In addition, each community action group was successful in implementing responsible beverage service training and most implemented compliance checks (to age-of-sale laws). Thus, in Project Northland, direct action strategies were seen as necessary to make changes at the community level in the norms that sustained adolescent alcohol use, because educational strategies and coalition building had not resulted in sufficient action or change.

Creating a Summary Grid of Potential Health Behavior Program Components

The program developer should make an exhaustive search for programs that have previously been developed concerning the selected health behavior. The descriptions and resources that were discussed in the preceding sections can be a starting point for those. Programs that have demonstrated success, that is, were able to change the targeted behavior or potent predictive factors, should be carefully reviewed. This will mean writing or calling the program developer or agency to obtain copies of the curricula, training manuals, intervention plans, and so forth. It is important to actually read and evaluate whether the components of the program are applicable to the targeted population and precisely what parts of the program were most likely to have contributed to its success.

If there are no evaluated programs for the health behavior selected, then reviewing other nonevaluated programs will provide the program developer with ideas for a health behavior program. It may also be useful to review highly successful programs, even if they are directed to another health behavior. There may be components of those programs that would be applicable to another behavior. In addition, the structure, length, and clarity of the program may have contributed to its success, and reviewing successful programs will provide models for how a health behavior program should be written.

The program developer can now make a large grid to summarize this review of health behavior programs. On the left side of the grid will be the intervention objectives. Across the top of the grid will be the types of health behavior programs: school-based, parent involvement, peer involvement, environmental change, and community action. Other types of programs that may not fit into these five categories can also be written across the top. From the review of the literature, then, the grid can be filled in with potential strategies to be part of the community-wide health behavior program. For example, in the WHO Study, role-playing of situations where there might be social pressure to drink were included in the curriculum. Thus, if the intervention objective for another program is to "increase self-efficacy to resist influences to drink," then under "School-Based Program" might be written "Classroom curriculum with role-playing, see WHO Study program." Not all of the squares in the grid need to be filled in, because some types of programs would not be applicable to some of the intervention strategies. However, it is useful to have at least two or more types of programs listed for each intervention objective so that there will be sufficient power to create change. An example of a grid from the intervention objectives in Table 3.2 is shown in Table 3.12. How the grid might be completed for just one of the columns, "School-Based Programs," is shown in Table 3.13. Although this is a somewhat time-consuming process, it will make much easier the stage of program writing, which will be discussed in the next chapter.

Once the grid is completed, it becomes much clearer as to the types of health behavior programs that will be selected. Some clearly can affect a greater number of the intervention objectives or do so more powerfully. Some programs may be the only ones able to achieve particular changes so must be included in the resulting program. At this point, a short summary can be written of each type of program that might optimally be included, and the pros and cons of each. A hierarchy of potential types of programs for the targeted group for the given health behavior can then be determined.

SUMMARY

This chapter described three steps in program development and sets the stage for determining, creating, and writing a program. Predictive factors were written as intervention objectives so that the outcomes of the health behavior program would be explicit. This is particularly important because a given predictive factor can be approached in multiple ways. The intervention objectives were written in simple and concise language. Then, the major types of health behavior programs for children and adolescents were

TABLE 3.12   A Summary Grid of Health Behavior Components by
Intervention Objective for Preventing the Onset of Smoking

	Type of Program				
Intervention Objective	*School-Based Programs*	*Parental Involvement*	*Peer Participation*	*Environmental Change*	*Community Action*
Increase numbers of adults and peers who are nonsmokers.					
Do not allow smoking at school.					
Promote having friends who do not like smoking.	(See Table 3.13)				
Teach ways to resist influences to smoke.					
Portray other activities as fun, mature, and so forth.					
Reduce expectations to smoke.					
Practice ways to promote nonsmoking.					
Practice ways to refuse.					

reviewed, including six types of school-based programs, five types of parent involvement programs, three types of peer involvement programs, examples of environmental change programs, and three types of community action approaches. For each of these, the advantages and disadvantages were outlined, resources were recommended, and how these types of programs have successfully been applied in my own research was discussed. Last, the creation of a grid that summarizes and ranks potential components of a health behavior program for each of the intervention objectives was described. Such a grid will guide the development of a program tailored to the selected behavior and targeted group.

TABLE 3.13   An Example of a Summary Grid of Potential School-Based
Program Components by Intervention Objective

Type of Program: School-Based Programs to Prevent the Onset of Smoking

Intervention Objectives	*Potential Components*
Increase adults and peers who are nonsmokers.	Curriculum—see Class of 1989 Study (Perry et al., 1992); use peer leaders to facilitate.
	Homework—see the Unpuffables (Elder et al., 1996) and Slick Tracy (Williams et al., 1995).
Do not allow smoking at school.	No smoking policy—see Pentz et al. (1989) and CATCH (Elder et al., 1996).
Promote having friends who do not like smoking.	Drug-free extracurricular activities (see Carnegie Council on Adolescent Development, 1992).
Teach ways to resist influences to smoke.	Curriculum—see Life Skills Training (Botvin et al., 1995).
Portray other activities as fun, mature, and so on.	Curriculum—see Class of 1989 Study. Drug-free extracurricular activities.
Reduce expectations to smoke.	Curriculum—see CLASP (McAlister et al., 1979) on ways to create goals to remain smoke free. Homework—see Slick Tracy.
Practice ways to promote nonsmoking.	Extracurricular activities—see SADD, Kick Butts, National Peer Helpers Network.
Practice ways to refuse.	Curriculum—see Class of 1989 Study and Life Skills Training Program

4

CREATING THE HEALTH BEHAVIOR PROGRAM

This chapter discusses Steps 7 and 8 in the program development process. The planning, review, and research that have been done in the previous steps are all put to use in the actual creation of a health behavior program. Up to this point, the process has been mostly a scientific one—careful review and analysis, with data-based decisions. The process of creating a health behavior program—of actually writing the components that make up a program—requires science and art, analysis and creativity, observation and intuition, education and entertainment. In this chapter, that process is described, including how to change intervention objectives into program components; assess what components are possible, powerful, and feasible; and to decide the presentation and packaging of the program. It is strongly advised, as was recommended in the last chapter, that previously successful health behavior programs be carefully reviewed to learn how they were written, presented, and packaged, to guide the writing of a new health behavior program.

STEP 7: CREATING PROGRAM COMPONENTS FROM INTERVENTION OBJECTIVES

This step is the part of program development that I find to be the most challenging—and the most fun. The program components must be created and considered in a way that will fit the mind-set of the target audience, attract their attention, engage them, and also powerfully change an intervention objective. The questions in Table 4.1 will guide this process.

TABLE 4.1 Step 7: Creating Program Components From Intervention Objectives

The following questions serve as a guide for creating potential program components:

1. Are there prior successful programs that are appropriate or that can be modified to meet an intervention objective?
2. Can a team be assembled of scientific, creative, and community-based people to consider how each intervention objective can be approached?
3. Is there a hierarchy of program components for the health behavior program? Which components are most likely to be effective?

A health behavior program does not need to be created from scratch because successful and powerful health behavior programs are increasingly available. Being able to implement an existing program saves time, money, and valuable resources. Thus, even if an existing program serves only part of the needs of a community-wide health behavior program, if it is appropriate, it should be strongly considered. The grid that was written in the previous step can serve as a guide.

For example, assume that the health behavior being addressed is young adolescent alcohol use and that one of the intervention objectives is to "increase the number of nondrinking peer role models." In reviewing the literature, there are several peer-led classroom curricula that have successfully reduced drinking among young adolescents by changing peer influence, including the Life Skills Training Program (Botvin et al., 1984) and Project Northland's "Amazing Alternatives!" program (Perry et al., 1996). Thus, if these existing curricula are appropriate to the targeted group, then they might be replicated. Copies of the curricula can be purchased, and these programs can be augmented by other components, such as community action or parent involvement.

If changes are needed in an existing successful program, then the original program developers should be contacted for their opinions on the revisions. For example, the role-play scenarios in the WHO Study were different for each of the four countries in the study so that the social situations portrayed in these scenarios were culturally appropriate and relevant. However, in all of the countries, role-plays were done, as this was seen as a necessary part of the program. Similarly, when the smoking prevention curriculum from the Class of 1989 Study was disseminated, many schools opted not to include the peer leader component, because it was unusual for schools and required additional personnel and expense. However, this is an essential component of the program, and the outcomes of the dissemination were not as powerful as what was expected from the earlier research (Murray et al., 1992). Thus, for changes that might be seen as needed, a discussion with the program developers might reveal whether the modifications will leave the program substantially less powerful and successful.

The Importance of a Creative Team

A creative and scientific team, with ample input and collaboration with community representatives, is essential to the process of creating a program. The creative people give humor, relevance, and life to a health behavior program, which may be essential in attracting the attention of young people. Creative people include those who regularly write materials for children (one can read their writings to assess how creative they are), who are involved with children's drama productions, who develop activities for young people at camps or in clubs, or who are involved in film productions for youth. The key elements in locating creative people are that they have previously developed materials for children and adolescents, that they have directly worked with young people, and that their work was well received by young people.

Once one or two creative people have been identified, a small team of creative people and the program developer(s) should work together. (Sometimes, program developers are also the creative people, but generally the program developers are the project coordinators or primary investigators.) The creative people can be introduced to the goal of the health behavior program and to the extensive review and research that was done in the previous steps. This is important because their creativity needs to fit within the project's objectives. Therefore, they should review the information on health consequences, epidemiology, and etiology. They should understand the meanings of the key predictive factors and that the health behavior program is guided by the intervention objectives.

Brainstorming sessions can then take place to consider each intervention objective and each type of program based on the grid previously developed. The brainstorming sessions should be open-ended in terms of types of approaches, but they should also be examined (by the program developer) as to their potential for meeting one of the intervention objectives. It is helpful if the group can consider several creative program ideas for each of the intervention objectives and type of health behavior program so that these ideas can be brought to the targeted group as well as community and multicultural representatives for their reactions and ideas.

Role Models

Some examples of how this process works might be helpful. In my earliest work with smoking prevention, I was interested in peer leaders as new role models of healthier behavior. Based on Bandura's (1977) research, the behavior of role models and the consequences of that behavior were primary ways in which people learn social behaviors, and we wanted to powerfully affect the types of role models that young adolescents were being exposed to concerning cigarette smoking. We selected high school students who applied to be peer leaders and were selected based on their written applications and interviews. The students selected were also those who we judged both looked and acted "cool" so that younger students would view them as viable role models (McAlister et al., 1980; McAlister, Perry, & Maccoby, 1979). The program was implemented in seventh-grade classrooms and was successful in reducing the onset of smoking up to 3 years after the intervention (Perry, Maccoby, & McAlister, 1980; Telch, Killen, McAlister, Perry, & Maccoby, 1982).

Because the use of role models had been successful in this study (and other smoking prevention efforts), we decided to incorporate healthy role models of eating and physical activity patterns into a curriculum for third-grade children. Because actual people, like parents, might not always eat healthfully or exercise regularly, we decided to create cartoon role models (from another planet—Planet Strongheart) who were devoted to health. These role models became the central characters in our curriculum "The Adventures of Hearty Heart and Friends" (Luepker et al., 1996; Perry et al., 1985). The main characters are shown in Figure 4.1. The characters became "larger than life" through a slide-tape adventure series, in which the characters discovered that life on the planet earth is not always conducive to heart health.

In Project Northland, we incorporated healthier role models in a number of ways. First, peer leaders led the classroom sessions and organized

Figure 4.1. The Main Characters of "The Adventures of Hearty Heart and Friends" from CATCH

SOURCE: Luepker et al. (1996). Used with permission.

Breathtest Mahoney and Slick Tracy

Figure 4.2. The Main Characters of "The Slick Tracy Home Team Program" from Project Northland
SOURCE: Perry et al. (1996). Used with permission.

activities outside of school (Komro, Perry, Veblen-Mortenson, et al., in press). Second, we created a series of comic books for the sixth graders, called "Slick Tracy," which featured two teenage detectives (Slick Tracy and Breathtest Mahoney) who were always trying to solve alcohol-related problems. In creating the booklets, the characters were first drawn by an artist to be adult detectives. In focus groups on the booklets, students felt the characters should be teens rather than adults. So Slick and Breathtest (as you can see in Figure 4.2) are about 14 or 15 years old and ride their bikes on all of their missions. (They were drawn as Caucasian teens because of the ethnic composition of the Project Northland communities.) Thus, they became viable role models and could provide clues about how to avoid or deal with alcohol-related situations. It should be noted that the Slick Tracy comic books also had "villains," and were full of puns and jokes that the students and adults found amusing, so the stories themselves were engrossing to the young adolescents (and their parents).

Third, in the "Amazing Alternatives!" curriculum that was implemented in the seventh grade in Project Northland, we created a teen soap opera based on four seventh-grade characters who had typical teen problems concerning alcohol use. The soap opera had eight parts—one for each classroom session—and was delivered by audiotapes to small groups in the classroom. The students could read the scripts as the audiotape was playing. Teenage actors recruited from a local theater company and arts high school created the audiotapes based on our scripts. The students found the soap opera very compelling—they even claimed that they knew who the characters were in real life! Because the characters modelled ways to avoid alcohol use and still be accepted by (or leaders of) the peer group, they were very powerful. Videotapes were considered, but the students reported in focus groups that they liked the audiotapes better than videotapes, as they were seen as different from other curricula that more frequently used videotapes.

Healthful role models can be introduced and reiterated throughout the multiple types of health behavior programs. Slick Tracy and Breathtest Mahoney, role models of "cool" nondrinking teens, were part of the peer-led classroom program, were the central characters in the home-based program, and served as an impetus for Slick Tracy Nights (where students displayed their own alcohol-related projects) in all of the Project Northland intervention communities. Thus, Slick Tracy and Breathtest Mahoney became role models in school, parent, peer, and community programs. By doing so, they became a motif or icon across the entire community that reinforced the norm of nondrinking for underage teens and were remembered even at high school graduation.

Skills Development

Traditionally, health education programs have emphasized knowledge acquisition but more recently, there has been an increased emphasis on skills development. This is based on the discrepancies between knowledge and behavior. For example, nearly all young adolescents know about the long-term consequences of smoking, yet many begin to smoke even with this knowledge (USDHHS, 1994). Similarly, in the Class of 1989 Study, we found that students had almost perfect knowledge of which foods in 18 food pairs was the "healthier" food. Yet, they usually chose to eat significantly fewer of the healthier foods (Perry, Kelder, & Klepp, 1994b). Part of the explanation for these discrepancies is that young people find the consequences of their behavior remote and irrelevant to them; they cannot really make an "informed" decision (Blum & Stark, 1985). Part of the explanation may also be that to enact a behavior requires a set of other behaviors—skills—which need to be learned before being able to regularly eat healthier foods or not smoke. Mastery of skills can lead to greater self-efficacy to perform the behavior, which in turn leads to enactment of the behavior (Bandura, 1986). Thus, skills development has become a central intervention objective in health behavior programs.

Skills development requires breaking down the behavior into its component parts in a way that is developmentally appropriate. For example, in Project Northland's "Amazing Alternatives!" program, seventh-grade students create role-plays concerning possible situations where they might be influenced to drink. We found that just asking students to create a role-play for a situation did not provide enough structure for them. In "Amazing Alternatives!," they first learned about various ways to respond to situations (see Table 4.2) and then identified these responses in the audiotapes of the four teens. The students practiced ways to respond to other situations within their small groups, then were given a script to complete and act out in front of their classmates. Table 4.3 is an example of one of these scripts. The skills of recognizing and responding to situations where young adolescents might be offered alcohol were (a) modeled by the peer leaders and characters on the audiotapes, (b) provided to the students with written examples, (c) rehearsed in dyads or small groups, and (d) performed in front of the class. This allowed each student to participate and practice these skills, as well as to model for other students, in the process.

Creating skills-building activities that involve parents is challenging because the program first needs to attract the attention of busy parents as well as motivate youth to participate with their parents. Our home team programs were successful in obtaining very high participation rates of parents or guardians and their children (generally over 70%), because the activities were embedded in homework assignments and structured so that each part of the assignment could be done in 10 to 15 minutes. In addition, parents and their child received points for each activity that was completed, and these points were recorded at school. Rewards were given for accrued points. An example of a skills-building activity from the Hearty Heart

TABLE 4.2   Worksheet on Skills to Resist Influences to Drink, From the "Amazing Alternatives!" Program From Project Northland

The "No's" Have It

There are so many different ways of saying *"No"* to offers of alcohol.
Here are just a few of those ways to successfully say "No."

Method	Offer	Example Response
No, thanks	"Do you want to have a drink?"	"No, thanks."
Something else going on	"Hey, I've got a six-pack—let's go get it."	"No way, but there's a great new movie I really want to see; let's go!"
There's my reason	"Do you want a bottle of this new wine cooler?"	"No, thanks; it makes people do stupid things."
Assert yourself	"Wanna drink?"	"That's 'no' for sure; I've made up my mind to not drink!" Then, just walk way.
No, no, a thousand times no	"How about a drink?" "Oh, come on, everyone's drinking!" "What are you worried about —you chicken?"	"No, thanks." "No, thanks." "No thanks, and not everyone is drinking."
Out of synch	"How about some beer?"	"No, it's just not me . . . I don't want to be known as a drinker."
Stand tall with friends (hang around with people who don't use alcohol)	"Let's go raid my parents' liquor cabinet."	"No way! None of my friends drink and neither do I!"
Stay away (stay away from places where you know people use alcohol)	"How about going down to the railroad tracks with me after school?"	"Are you kidding? All people ever do there is drink and go crazy . . . it's a bad scene!"

SOURCE: Perry et al. (1996). Used with permission.

Home Team program, part of CATCH, is shown in Table 4.4, where parents and their children set goals to eat less salt.

TABLE 4.3   Role Play Script From the "Amazing Alternatives!" Program
From Project Northland

Role-Play Script #1: Bad News Barbecue			
Roles: Peer Leader	Friend #1	Friend #4	For a smaller group,
	Friend #2	Friend #5	combine Friends #1 and #2
	Friend #3	Jessica	or Friends #3 and #5 or both.

Peer Leader: This scene takes place at Jessica's house. She is in her living room with some of her friends. Outside, in the backyard, her older sister, Kelly, is having a barbecue with some of her friends.

(Jessica and her friends are looking out the window at the older kids)

Friend #1:	Wow, Jessica! Your sister sure has a lot of friends!
Jessica:	I don't know. I've never seen a lot of these kids before!
Friend #2:	Gee, look at the hair on that guy! It's purple!
Friend #3:	(Pointing) Look at her (him)! With the red striped shirt! He (she) is really cute!
Friend #4:	Hey look! Those two guys just brought in some beer!
Jessica:	Oh-oh, Kelly's really gonna be in trouble now. My parents are gonna be home pretty soon.
Friend #5:	Let's get something to eat. I could eat that whole bowl of chips out there.
Jessica:	Well, I don't know. I'd have to ask Kelly if she would mind.
Friend #2:	Mind! She wouldn't even notice! There are so many people out there!
Friend #3:	(sigh) I wish the red-striped shirt would notice!
Friend #4:	I'll bet she wouldn't notice if we took some of that beer, either, what do you think, you guys?
Jessica:	(Choose a "No" technique.) _____
Friend #4:	C'mon, who is going to notice?
Jessica:	(Use "No, no, a thousand times no" technique.) _____
Friends #1, 2, 3, and 5:	(Join in saying "no." Come up with an alternative.)
	_____
Friend #4:	(Agree with other kids and alternative.) _____

SOURCE: Perry et al. (1996). Used with permission.

Skills development is also critical to include in health behavior programs aimed at changes in the larger social environment. Adults, for example, need to learn skills to be able to organize their communities, which in turn affect the health of young people. These skills—being able to assess their communities, create a viable action team, develop media advocacy concerning their health behavior, maintain momentum on an issue, write new

TABLE 4.4   Skills Development Activity From the "Hearty Heart Home Team" Program from CATCH

ACTIVITY 3

Adult Points: 1   Kid Points: 1

Now try goal-setting to help your team cut down on salt! Look at this week's Team Tips for ideas of changes you could make. Try to take the salt shaker off the table for at least one week and then decide on one other goal your team would like to work on during the next week. Write your goal here and "GOAL FOR IT!"

1. *We will take the salt shaker off the*
   table for at least one week.

2. _____

   _____

   _____

   _____

Score 2 points for setting
and reaching your team's goal.

TABLE 4.5   Skills to Plan Alcohol-Free Activities, From the "Peer Participation" Program From Project Northland

---

Deciding on What to Eat

1. Theme: Is there a party theme? If so, do you want the food to fit with the theme?
2. Think simple: Finger food and soft drinks are the best way to go.
3. Timing: Will the food be served during the entire event or just at a specific time?
4. Buying the food: Will local merchants or fast-food restaurants donate anything? Make a list of sources for donations.
5. Assign someone to be in charge of the food: The help of the adviser will be appreciated here.
6. Preparing and serving the food: How much will it take? How many adult volunteers are needed? Remember to think simple.
7. Equipment or utensils: What equipment will be needed to store, prepare, and serve food?
8. Cost: How much will it cost? How much can you spend?
9. Purchasing: Who will purchase the food? When will it be purchased? Whoever volunteers to purchase food should contact the Project Northland Coordinator.

SOURCE: Perry et al. (1996). Used with permission.

policies for their communities, and communicate the need for changes in policies and practices—need to be anticipated and learned by organizers for direct action community organizing to be successful (Blaine et al., 1997; Forster et al., 1998). Even a seemingly "easy" program, the peer participation program in Project Northland, which involved young people in the seventh and eighth grades planning and implementing their own alcohol-free social activities, required skills development (Komro et al., 1994). The training program for the peer participation program, in addition to motivational activities such as the appearance of basketball players from the nearby university, involved breaking a "party" down into its component parts and learning about what decisions needed to be made. The peer participation program leaders learned about deciding who to invite, choosing party activities, choosing a party site, deciding on the party hours, designing the party schedule, deciding on what to eat (see Table 4.5), figuring out what is needed, figuring out how much the party will cost, setting up party rules, getting the word out, and cleaning up. This skills development was done through small group discussions and reports during the training, so the students were able to begin to plan alternative activities directly following the training. As a result, the students successfully implemented alcohol-free activities, which resulted in lower drinking rates among the planners (Komro et al., 1996).

Summary of Program Components

These few examples of program components show how intervention objectives were approached in previously successful health behavior programs, with the input of a variety of creative people. The program developer can use these resources and add new creative components by assembling a creative team and considering each of the intervention objectives and type of program. The result will be the grid developed at the end of the last chapter (Tables 3.12 and 3.13) but now, with the proposed program components written in each part of the grid.

For example, in Table 3.13, for the intervention objective "increase adults and peers who are nonsmoking," the table referred to the Unpuffables and Slick Tracy programs as examples of programs designed to involve parents. Because the Unpuffables program was written for fifth-grade students and because Slick Tracy was developed around alcohol use, neither of the programs is directly applicable to young adolescent smoking prevention. Thus, the creative team might decide to develop a new home team program for young adolescents and their parents and would spend some time brainstorming and discussing how to do this. The new summary program component grid might now say next to "increase adults and peers who are nonsmoking,"

> Create a new home team program called the 'SmokeOuts,' with four teenage characters as role models, an adventure story, and activities for the students to complete with their parents on the consequences of teenage smoking, second-hand smoking, advertising and promotional activities, peer influences, and family rules about smoking.

Once the grid has been completed (and again, not all of the squares may be able to be filled in), then the task of prioritizing begins. The primary concern at this point is to identify those program components that are most likely to be able to change a predictive factor and meet an intervention objective. Therefore, for each intervention objective, the two program components that are most potent (able to change a predictive factor) and able to reach a large percentage of the targeted population should be identified. (They can be circled in red pencil on the grid, for example.) Because there should be about 10 to 15 intervention objectives (from the selected predictive factors), this process outlines about 20 to 30 of the most powerful program components (selecting from school, parent, peer, environmental, community action, or other program types) that will form the basis of the health behavior program.

A summary of this process should be written. Because some of the program components will use the same type of program, and therefore will be implemented together, these should be noted. For example, a peer-led classroom program can be designed to meet several intervention objectives, including changing role models, developing skills, creating new norms, and so on. A program type that is able to address several intervention objectives will not only be more powerful but more efficient as well. This will be particularly crucial to maximize the resources that are available. The summary of program components should therefore include the program type, intervention objectives to be met, and the description of the program component that has come from the creative team. An example of a potential smoking prevention program is shown in Table 4.6.

The potential smoking prevention program includes these elements:

- A peer-led smoking prevention curriculum
- After-school activities planned by youths
- New school smoking policies or the enforcement of school rules
- A home team program
- A parent night with student-created projects
- Peer involvement in the classroom, after-school, and on action teams
- A pledge-not-to-smoke contest supported by posters, postcards, and mass media
- The formation of a community action team to consider policies to support nonsmoking among youths

Note that these are the proposed or potential components. They were selected because they were seen as potentially powerful in making changes in the intervention objectives, were potent in prior prevention programs, and were seen as appropriate for the targeted group by the creative, scientific, and community-based team members.

TABLE 4.6   An Example of a Summary of Potential Program Components

Tentative program title: "The SmokeOuts"

Behavioral goal: To reduce the onset of smoking among young adolescents

Program Components

Program Type:	Intervention Objectives (from Table 3.12)	Description (from Creative Team)
School-based	Increase numbers of adults & peers who are nonsmokers.	Six-session peer-led curriculum from Class of 1989 Study; revise to include audiotapes like those used in "Amazing Alternatives!"
	Teach skills to resist influences to smoke.	Revised 6-session curriculum from Class of 1989 Study.
	Practice ways to refuse.	Include in revised curriculum.
	Promote having friends who do not like smoking.	After-school activities planned by students; use Project Northland peer program.
	Portray other activities as fun, mature, and so forth.	Include in curriculum and after-school activities.
	Practice ways to promote nonsmoking.	Include in curriculum and after-school activities.
	Do not allow smoking at school.	Revise school policies based on CATCH, and enforce rules.
Parent involvement	Increase numbers of adults & peers who are nonsmokers.	Four-session "SmokeOuts" home team program implemented after the curriculum.
	Teach skills to resist influences to smoke.	SmokeOut Night with students displaying smoking-related projects.
Peer involvement	Increase numbers of adults & peers who are nonsmokers.	Peer leadership training for curriculum.
	Practice ways to promote nonsmoking.	Peer involvement in planning after-school activities.
	Promote having friends who do not like smoking.	Include in peer involvement in planning after-school activities.
	Reduce expectations to smoke.	Peer participation in action teams.
Environmental	Reduce expectations to smoke.	Poster and postcard campaign with pledge-not-to-smoke contest.
		Mass media (TV, radio, news) to support contest.
Community	Increase numbers of adults & peers who are nonsmokers.	Form community action teams to promote nonsmoking for the whole community based on Project Northland methods.

TABLE 4.7   Step 8: Constructing the Health Behavior Program

The following questions guide the process of constructing a health behavior program:

1. What resources are available for the health behavior program? Who will conduct the program? Are there available settings? What are the anticipated costs? Will others collaborate? Is there ample time to write the new components?

2. How are the program components written? What style? How should they be packaged?

3. Are the program components culturally and developmentally appropriate for the targeted audience? Do they attract their attention, engage them, fit their mind-sets?

STEP 8: CONSTRUCTING THE
HEALTH BEHAVIOR PROGRAM

The health behavior program is ready to be finalized and written. This step involves the balance between what is optimal (the final grid at the end of the last step) and what is feasible. The program should be creative and engaging but also able to be implemented. Table 4.7 provides the questions that guide this step.

Resources

The availability of resources is critical in the program development process. The primary resources that need to be considered are money, personnel, time, collaborations, and settings. These types of resources are needed to create the program, implement the program, and maintain the program. (Resources also are needed to evaluate the program, and those will be discussed in the next chapter.) A summary of the types of resources needed is provided in Table 4.8.

The amount of money needed depends on how many program components are being created, the number of young people in the targeted group, the types of program components (because some are more expensive to create and implement than others), and the number of people available to work on program creation and implementation. Personnel are needed to create program activities and accompanying artwork, put them into an acceptable package using desktop publishing or audio-visual-computer technologies, train appropriate program implementors, and facilitate implementation and maintenance. Each of the program components should be reviewed and then have a cost attached to it, based on the money and

TABLE 4.8   Types of Resources Needed for the Creation and Implementation of a Health Behavior Program

Resources	Program Creation	Program Implementation and Maintenance
Money	Training manual design	Manual components—binder, paper, dividers, and so on
	Original artwork	Copies of manuals, activities, and artwork
	Student activity sheets	Copies of student materials
	Audiovisuals	Media duplication costs
	Meeting costs for site, food, materials	Training costs for site, food, stipends
	Pilot tests and focus groups	Equipment and food
	Program brochures	Mailing and postage
		Media distribution (advertising, PSAs, etc.)
Personnel	Creative writers	Trainers for teachers, peer leaders, community action teams
	Artists for design	People to implement the program or facilitate
	Desk-top publishing	People who will work to maintain the program
	Program developer	
	Mailings	
Time	Writing	Classroom time
	Artwork	After-school time
	Pilot testing	Parent availability
	Focus groups	Training time
	Needs assessments	Action team development time
Collaborations and sites	School districts	School districts
	Parent-teacher organizations	Parent-teacher organizations
	Existing task forces or coalitions	Existing task forces or coalitions
	Community leaders	Community leaders
	Community groups	Community groups
	Parks and recreation departments	Parks and recreation departments

personnel that will be needed. Generally, it is better to scale back the number of program components than to try to scale back the needed resources for any given component. For example, there are considerable costs in printing home team booklets for each child and parent, especially if they are in color. Some modifications might be acceptable, such as printing on colored paper or just having the booklet covers in attractive colors. However, if the number of pages are reduced by making the print very small or eliminating pictures, then the materials may become unattractive and will lose their appeal to the targeted audience.

Time is also a resource that is needed to carefully create each component and to ensure that ample time is available for implementation. A rule of thumb for our groups is that it takes a full year to develop a multicomponent health behavior program for one grade level concerning one behavior. This year is spent going through all the steps presented in this book, including at least one full pilot test with the targeted group. Similarly, training sessions are generally 1 to 2 full days at a time, during the work week, and with stipends for the trainees (to cover teacher substitutes, extra time, etc.). Training sessions that occur when people are tired or on the weekends are a burden to the trainees, because the training takes away from their families and free time. There also needs to be enough time to implement the program. This is an issue in schools, for example, where classroom time is at a premium, and parents and school personnel want that time to be productive. Generally, a classroom program that has six to eight 45-minute sessions has been the longest we can negotiate with a large number of schools. Therefore, if a health behavior program is designed to be 20 sessions long, it may not be feasible to implement in many schools. Time is also a factor for parents and adults involved in the programs, given their generally busy schedules. The program developer needs to consider how best to fit into their time schedules (rather than having them fit into our time schedule). This means bringing the programs to them and making the time both productive and engaging.

Last, to accomplish a community-wide health behavior program, collaborations need to be developed. For a school-based program, collaboration with the school district(s) is necessary, because without the school district's permission, no program will be implemented. It is useful to begin to talk with collaborators once the type of program components have been decided. The school district, for example, may insist that someone from their curriculum and instruction staff review or provide input into the program or be part of the creative team. The district might put limits on how many sessions can be implemented, by which teachers, and when in the school year. For community programs, collaborations with community leaders, businesses, and community agencies will facilitate implementation. In some communities, existing coalitions and task forces may already address some aspect of the health behavior, and working on how to formally join efforts can be fruitful. Last, sites for implementing a program component should be clarified. This is usually done through collaborations, but sometimes, a site will need to be rented or its availability determined prior to proceeding.

The necessary resources—money, personnel, time, collaborations, sites—should be clarified before finally deciding on the components of a health behavior program. The program developer can go back to the summary of proposed program components and intervention objectives and based on the assessment of resources, decide which of the program components will be developed. This process will ensure that the final product will be able to be implemented, because the costs associated with it and the people to create it have all been determined to be adequate.

Constructing the Health Behavior Program

Constructing the health behavior program consists of creating the individual components as well as a synergistic package. Generally, after deciding which program components will be created, an overall theme or motif for the program is developed. This theme or motif serves to connect the various program components and to give the program an identity. For example, we decided on the name "Project Northland: Partnerships for Youth Health" for the overall project, because it was to be implemented in northern Minnesota (which is considered the northland) and because we were determined to create partnerships with the communities in the study. We did not include the term "alcohol" in the project name because we wanted the primary purpose of our programs—youth health promotion—to be given priority and because of some people's strong reactions to alcohol-related efforts. In addition, each year of Project Northland had a motif to tie together the various program components. For the seventh grade, this was "Amazing Alternatives!" This was the name of the peer-led classroom program. We also had an Amazing Alternatives! Home Program for parents and an Amazing Alternatives! Awesome Autumn Party for parents and seventh graders. Students and community task forces also planned alternative activities for their peers, so the theme was carried through all of the program components. In addition to the themes, a visual image is generally created for program materials. For the "Amazing Alternatives!" program, this was a maze, signifying the many choices that young adolescents make on their way to adulthood.

The program components are then written, with one or two programs generally being central to the health behavior program, such as the classroom-based curricula in the Class of 1989 Study, the community action teams during the second phase of Project Northland, or the theater production "2 Smart 2 Smoke" in an ongoing project with the Allina Health System and the National Theatre for Children (Komro, Perry, Williams et al., in press; Perry et al., 1994a; Perry, Komro et al., in press). The central program(s) is or are written first so that the other components can be created to be complementary. Thus, the health behavior program is built. The necessary parts of each program component are first outlined and reviewed by the creative team, then drafted by the creative writer based on the brainstorming sessions of the creative team, and again reviewed by a wider team. The potential parts of various types of programs are shown in Table 4.9.

Although a creative and scientific team does the brainstorming to determine the program components, themes, and motifs, generally one or two people do the actual creation or writing of the program. This allows for continuity in the writing style and a similar voice throughout the program. For a classroom curriculum, for example, the writer will first outline the entire curriculum, including the total number of sessions, length (minutes) of each session, topics for each session, audio-visual-computer components, and main theme or motif. After this has been reviewed by the creative team, then the writer will prepare one or two sessions, which serve as model sessions for the curriculum. These are reviewed by the creative team; then, the writer can complete the curriculum with the same style and approach. During this time, the writer may need to begin working with an artist for accompanying artwork and with the person who does desktop publishing, to begin to put together the draft program.

Of major importance in the writing of the program components is a clear, simple, and detailed presentation. The language should be easily understood by the targeted group. However, the more detailed, complete, and user-friendly the presentation, the easier the program will be to implement. Everything that the program developer expects the person who will implement the program to do or say should be explicitly written. An early worry I had was that this would be insulting to teachers, community leaders, and

TABLE 4.9   Types of Health Behavior Programs and Potential Components

School-based programs	Teacher manuals of classroom activities
	Peer leader manuals of classroom activities
	Peer leader manuals for after-school programs
	Student activity worksheets and homework
	Audiotapes and videotapes
	Computer games and web sites
	Teacher training protocols
	Peer leader training protocols
	School food service staff manuals
	School food service staff training protocols
	Snack preparation and taste testing recipes
	School policy manuals
	Theater productions
	Incentives and rewards
	School and classroom posters
	Contest materials
Family involvement	Home team adventure stories
	Home team activity books
	Home team implementation manuals
	Home team incentives, rewards, posters
	Postcards and mailed information
	Parent educational program manual
	Parent educational program materials
	Recipes and activities for families
	Parent home visits scripts and materials
Peer involvement	Peer leader and counselor training manual
	Peer action team training manual
	Peer leader and counselor resource manual
	Peer action group activity manual
Environmental change	Recipes and nutritional information cards
	Menu modification manual
	Social marketing and counteradvertising materials
	Direct action organizing manual
Community action	Media advocacy manuals
	Community organizing training manual
	Direct action organizing manual
	Slide presentations on health behavior
	Information on potential policies and practices
	Storyboards

even peer leaders. What we have found over many years is that program
facilitators appreciate the details of the instructions, that they can modify

TABLE 4.10   Instructions to Teachers From "The Adventures of Hearty
Heart and Friends" From CATCH

Activity 2: Hearty Heart Adventure Story

Purpose: To view the first Hearty Heart episode and then identify
and discuss some of the important points in the adventure.

A. Announce to the class that every week during "Hearty Heart," they will see adventure stories about Hearty Heart and his friends, all of whom they read about during the first class.

B. Instruct students to prepare to watch "Episode 1: Hearty Goes on a Mission," by putting aside everything on their desks and being good listeners. (be sure to explain that the definition of *episode* means "part," so today's "Episode 1" is "Part 1.")

C. Show Episode 1. (There is a script of the episode at the end of this session.)

(Synopsis: Hearty Heart accepts a mission to go to Planet Earth to find the children who wrote Principal Goodheart asking for information about what they needed to know to prepare to visit Planet Strongheart. Hearty invites his friends Dynamite Diet, Salt Sleuth, and Flash Fitness to help him with this mission. As Hearty and his friends prepare to blast off for Earth, they explain that healthful eating and exercise are both important to heart health.)

D. Discuss the adventure story, as time permits.

  Ask:

> • *Where is Hearty Heart from?* (Planet Strongheart)
> • *Why is he being sent on a mission?* (Some children on Earth wrote to Mr. Good-heart, the principal of his school, asking for information on heart health so that they could prepare to visit Planet Strongheart.)
> • *Who did Hearty Heart invite to go along with him to Earth?* (Dynamite Diet, Salt Sleuth, and Flash Fitness)

SOURCE: Luepker et al. (1996). Used with permission.

them if they choose, but they can rely on having the exact wording if needed. This also makes it easier for the program to be conducted by a substitute facilitator and generally requires less preparation time for already-trained facilitators. Table 4.10 provides an example of this from CATCH's "Hearty Heart & Friends" curriculum for third-grade students. These are instructions for watching and discussing the first Hearty Heart adventure story. Note that what the teacher might say is written in italics after each part of the activity.

In addition to being detailed and precise, the program components should be user-friendly, attractive, and practical. Therefore, a participants' or trainers' manual should be written clearly and precisely, but it should also be easy to follow and contain all of the needed items. The learner objectives, what the targeted group should learn or be able to do following the program, should be stated at the beginning of each program component. The manuals are also divided up by time, sessions, or subject for ease of implementation. Additional resources are included in the manual itself, rather than expecting the implementer to prepare them. These include overhead transparencies as well as scripts of audio-visual materials and copies of handouts. To facilitate this, our manuals and materials are generally put together in three-ring binders that have pockets on the front and back covers. These binders can be divided, and examples of materials such as incentives or charts can be stored in the pockets. The three-ring binder makes it possible to subsequently add to the program should additional resources become available.

The program should be as easy to implement as possible; by creating a program in this way, it is much more likely to be implemented as planned. The program components should also be attractive to the targeted group. The use of neon-colored paper with young children, or comic book adventure stories with young adolescents, or professionally made videos with older teens have all been successful in prior programs, in part, because the targeted groups found them to be something worth their attention. Given the competing media and materials available to youth, it becomes even more important that health-related materials be sophisticated and appealing.

The programs should also be practical, that is, they should be able to be implemented under usual circumstances in schools, at home, or in the community. This does not mean that new approaches should be discarded but only that they need to fit the practicalities of the settings in which they will be implemented. For example, we replaced older peer leaders with same-age peer leaders in our smoking prevention programs primarily because it was much easier and more reliable to recruit and train peers who were in the same classrooms and schools. We also continue to have students prepare healthy snacks, but these snacks are simple enough to easily prepare in the classroom and can be managed by a teacher and the food service staff. Therefore, consideration of how the program will fit in the usual settings and circumstances is important during the creative process.

Focus Groups and Pilot Testing

In Chapter 3, we discussed the use of focus groups to determine how the targeted group perceives the intervention objectives. The same process can be used during the creation of a program component, particularly when novel approaches are being designed. The focus groups can provide feedback on various approaches, messages, and content prior to committing resources to develop the program. For example, we use focus groups before writing a home team adventure story to make sure that the story and main characters were appealing. We get reactions to postcard messages, to look for unanticipated responses to them. We invite children to sample foods from new recipes before proposing changes in the school food service. Small groups of the targeted group can provide fairly rapid feedback that might save considerable program development resources.

Once the drafts of the program components have been completed, a pilot of the program should be conducted. This ensures that the program will appeal to the targeted audience, that each activity that has been designed is appropriate, that training of those implementing the programs is adequate, and that the practical details of the program are all reviewed. For school-based programs, a school in the targeted community or similar to the targeted community can be recruited to serve as the pilot school. For parent involvement programs, generally 10 to 15 parents of the targeted age group are recruited. The environmental change programs can be implemented on a small scale at first, then expanded as they prove feasible and effective. For each of the pilots, the entire program is implemented, including drafts of audio-visual-computer materials, if applicable.

Observations of the pilot test implementation is critical—the program developer or writer or other members of the creative team should observe as much of the pilot implementation as possible. The observations verify that each activity is able to be implemented as planned and that the targeted group participates and favorably responds to it. After the pilot test implementation, interviews should take place with those who implemented the program and those who received it, such as students, teachers, parents, and community leaders. After the pilot test, revisions to the program components can take place, based on what did or didn't work during the pilot phase. The program components are then ready for final production and packaging for implementation.

SUMMARY

This chapter discussed how intervention objectives become program components, which in turn become the health behavior program. The importance of working with creative people in the creation of programs for young people is stressed. The resulting programs are more appealing, interesting, attractive, engaging, and in tune with the mind-set of young people. The creative team works together to decide on program components, both those that have previously been developed and new components. The program components are created by one or two individuals to ensure continuity across the program, but the components are reviewed by the entire creative and scientific team. The program components should be simply written or prepared with attention to detail, so that those who implement the program know exactly what to say and do. The program components should be attractive to the targeted group and user-friendly. They should be able to be implemented under usual circumstances. To test how new and innovative approaches will be received by the targeted groups, focus groups can be conducted. A pilot of all of the program components should be undertaken with a portion of the targeted group or a similar group, with observations and interviews of the pilot implementation and with those who participate in it. The final program components can then be revised and are ready for more widespread implementation.

5

IMPLEMENTING AND MAINTAINING A HEALTH BEHAVIOR PROGRAM

This chapter addresses the final two steps in the program development process. After the health behavior program has been created, that is, after the program components have been finalized and coordinated with each other with an overall theme or motif, pilot tested, and revised based on the pilot test, then the program is ready for implementation. The implementation process is crucial to the success of any health behavior program. Even the most creative, involving, and motivating program will not have an effect if it is only partially or inadequately implemented. Likewise, it is important to consider how the health behavior program will be maintained after its initial implementation so that even if the program is successful, it doesn't end up shelved or discontinued. In addition, this chapter addresses some final considerations and provides a short summary of the 10 steps and a checklist of what should be accomplished at each step. Reasons for unsuccessful programs are also presented, with possible remedial steps. This brings the program developer back to the beginning, with new skills to initiate a new health behavior program or strengthen the existing one.

STEP 9: IMPLEMENTING COMMUNITY-WIDE HEALTH BEHAVIOR PROGRAMS

Many of the questions concerning the implementation of the health behavior program may have already been addressed prior to this stage in the development process. For example, if a school district decides to develop a new nutrition curriculum, then the district has most likely decided what teachers will teach it and how many hours of class time to devote to it and

TABLE 5.1   Step 9: Implementing Community-Wide Health Behavior Programs

The following questions provide a framework for addressing how programs are implemented:

1. Has the health behavior program been introduced to key people for approval or support? Have written agreements been obtained?
2. Are the training programs sufficient to ensure implementation with high fidelity?
3. Can problems in implementation be anticipated, recorded, and remedied?
4. Is there a systematic process to report progress to the community and to make revisions?

considered issues of training. In the assessment of resources discussed in the previous chapter, discussions with key people in the community may have already taken place, to plan for costs, personnel, time, collaborations, and sites. Thus, the process described here includes components of implementation and some may take place earlier in the development process. The primary questions guiding this step are shown in Table 5.1.

Introductory Meetings With Key Community Members

When the health behavior program can be clearly described, then it is important to meet with the key people in the community who will support or help implement the program. With school-based programs, this should occur once decisions have been made on the major components of the program but prior to the creation of the actual program components. For example, in the first phase of Project Northland, we had already decided on classroom curricula in Grades 6 through 8: a parent involvement program in sixth grade, peer leadership in seventh grade, and community task forces for 3 years, when we met with representatives from 30 school districts in northeastern Minnesota (over a 6-week period). In those meetings, we presented the goals, rationale, and overview of the program. In Project Northland, this was done by a 10-minute video, followed by a verbal presentation. We provided a short summary of our previous work to establish credibility. We negotiated the number of classroom hours that could be devoted to the program, teacher training schedules, office space for Project Northland staff, and other resources, in addition to seeking approval to conduct a large community trial (Perry, Williams et al., 1993).

The meetings were first arranged with the school district superintendent. We encouraged the superintendent to invite other school district administrators, counselors, school principals, teachers, parents, students, and other school staff. A key component of these meetings was to stress how the schools would benefit from the program and exactly how much it would cost for them to participate. The conclusion of this meeting process was a participation agreement, a written document of what was expected of the schools and the program developers. Thus, to be prepared for these school meetings, the program developer should have a very good idea of what the program components will consist of (number of sessions, length of sessions, costs, training needed, etc.) prior to these meetings but also be able to allow leeway for input by the school district.

For parental and peer involvement programs, meetings can be held with representative organizations, such as parent-teacher organizations, Boy or Girl Scouts, 4H, faith organizations, and the like. If the programs are to take place at school, then they are considered, in part, school-based programs, and the school district needs to approve the programs. For environmental change programs, meetings might include grocery retailers, restaurateurs, community parks and recreation managers, and media and advertising agencies.

For community organization efforts, the process of "meeting" the community is often the first step in implementation of the health behavior program. The community organizer or community coordinator arranges meetings (one-on-one) with key community leaders and people in the various sectors (business, government, schools, media, law enforcement, faith organizations) and then presents the goals of the community- organizing efforts (such as new policies or practices in the community concerning underage drinking). The meetings serve as a gauge of community support for these goals and to identify those community members who might be active supporters and participants on task forces and action teams. In Project Northland, the organizers conducted about 100 such meetings in their communities (with fewer in the smaller communities) to initiate the second phase of the project (Komro, Perry, Williams, et al., in press).

Clearly, meetings with key people in the community are necessary and important for the success of a health behavior program. Often, community members are the people to initiate a health behavior program. Because these are generally small groups of people, the same process of program development still applies, and meetings with others in the community who are needed for their support or for implementation will still be necessary. Therefore, it is still important for the program developer to have clear goals, a rationale for the program, key facts on the health behavior (as was described in Chapter 2), what has been done before, and what the health behavior program will entail. The program developer will need to stress multiple benefits of the program—for young people, the community, the specific organization—and how they outweigh the costs, to rally support, enthusiasm, and collaboration for the health behavior program.

Training

Most health behavior programs involve new information, skills, approaches, and activities for those who will implement them. Although training books and videos can be made to introduce new information and skills, face-to-face training is more likely to yield greater compliance to a program (Perry, Murray, & Griffin, 1990). As mentioned earlier, we try to arrange training sessions during the normal work day and compensate those who attend or arrange substitutes for teachers. Attending a training program in the evening or on the weekend may decrease attendance and can be a burden on the trainee. Whenever possible, costs for teacher substitutes or compensation for their time should be arranged. The training should be designed to be active, interesting, pleasant, informative, and skills building. Trainers should be enthusiastic and energetic, as well as competent. There should be ample time to present the goals and objectives of the program, a convincing rationale for conducting the program with the targeted group in that community, an overview of the program and program manual, and details on each component and activity. The training should include the active participation of those involved. Thus, even though there is quite a lot of information to impart, it is more effective if training methods are considered so that the participants remain actively involved. The major components of health behavior training programs are outlined in Table 5.2.

There are excellent resources to guide the design of effective training programs. Among these is Kroehnert's (1995) *Basic Training for Trainers,* which provides practical information on developing training programs, including the principles of adult learning, types of methods of instruction,

TABLE 5.2   Components of Health Behavior Training Programs

Enthusiastic and competent trainers
Sufficient time during the normal work day
Structured activities to meet other trainees and regular breaks to ensure a safe and sociable setting
Snacks and food
A clear presentation of the health behavior goal and rationale for the program
Using active learning methods as much as possible in teaching the content of the program
Modelling of the program's components by the trainer
Active participation by the trainee in essential activities included in the program
Rehearsal of the program's components by the trainee
Allowing the trainee to "teach" part of the training program
Developing an implementation plan with potential for feedback or observation
Evaluation of the training by the trainees

ways to handle difficult situations, training aids, and training budgets. Silberman's (1998) *Active Training* offers invaluable information on developing effective training components. Qualities of active training are discussed in this book, including (a) a moderate level of content; (b) balancing affective, behavioral, and cognitive learning; (c) using a variety of learning approaches; (d) providing opportunities for group participation; (e) using participants' experience; (f) incorporating previously learned concepts and skills; (g) emphasizing real-world problem solving; and (h) allowing for future planning. These qualities help in the retention of information and motivation to comply with the program's protocol (Silberman, 1998).

For a classroom curriculum, for example, several lessons can be modeled by the trainer, then subsequent lessons prepared and presented by the participants. Those being trained should have ample time to rehearse the various components of the health behavior program so that they understand how the manual will work for them and where all the support materials are located and so that they feel confident in being able to present the health behavior program. The final part of the training should include making an implementation plan, including the dates when various sessions will be taught or activities completed and what is needed to prepare or accomplish these activities. It is useful for the program developer to schedule a time to observe or meet with each of those being trained at the training; this provides motivation for the person being trained to begin to implement the program.

For peer leader training, young people are also trained during the school day, if possible. For a four-session program, the training will be about 2 hours. For more demanding programs, such as the peer action teams in Project Northland, full day retreats were scheduled. The trainings with young people need to be even more active and participatory than with adults but with the same components. The peer leaders should leave the training knowing when they will implement the program, having practiced most of the program's components, and feeling confident about their ability to implement it. Protocols for training of peer leaders should look very much like teachers' instructions in a curriculum—detailed, user-friendly, explicit, and complete. These written instructions provide an excellent record and facilitate subsequent maintenance or expansion of the program, particularly because peer leaders are often an unusual or unfamiliar program component.

For community action training, the principles of organizing can be explained, with skills development focusing on conducting one-on-one interviews, community analyses, and team building. The health behavior being targeted also is a focus of these trainings, particularly as possible community-level policies and practices are discussed, prior experiences in other communities shared, and the steps to gather support and change policies are outlined. For example, the development of community policies to reduce alcohol use among youths requires specific knowledge concerning alcohol laws and policies.

After the initial training sessions, several other types of training opportunities are important for successful community organizing. The first involves the experiences of other community organizers. This can be accomplished by scheduling and facilitating sharing and problem-solving sessions. In addition, regular updates by organizers via E-mails to an entire group provides valuable insights from peers in a timely manner. The second training approach involves site visits, where the program developer or a more senior, experienced organizer works with an organizer on site or with an action team, to discuss strategies and next steps. Because each community setting is unique, these more individualized training opportunities facilitate personalized learning and action. The third training opportunity can be through written documents or web sites. For example, Join Together has an excellent web site for those interested in taking action concerning drug use and violence (http://www.jointogether.org). This web site is updated daily and has links to new resources and insights from others doing similar work. Because community action programs are not set, like a curriculum is, developing a more flexible and personalized training program greatly facilitates the implementation process. Each training includes an evaluation by the trainees. Generally, this is written feedback on the various components of the training as well as questions concerning the trainees' perceptions of the importance of the program and their confidence in being able to implement the program's components.

Implementation Evaluation

Being able to document what took place during the implementation of a health behavior program is perhaps as important as assessing outcomes. If a health behavior program is shown to work, that is, to change behavior, then understanding how the program was implemented is important in determining what it was that worked. King, Morris, and Fitz-Gibbon (1987) note in their very practical book, "How to Assess Program Implementation," that assessing implementation is important for accountability, for creating a lasting description of the program, and for providing a list of the possible causes of the program's effects. In addition, if the health behavior program is to continue, then it can be improved through careful monitoring of implementation (Patton, 1997).

Each component of a health behavior program and its implementation can be included in implementation evaluation (also referred to as process evaluation). Records can be reviewed that document meetings and communication with key people who were needed to support or implement a program. Training programs can be observed to record whether the programs included all the specified, necessary components. Those who participated in training can report their impressions of the training and whether it was sufficient for them to feel confident in implementing the program. The actual implementation of a program can be observed by the program developer or trained observers. Feedback on components of the program can be obtained by those who implemented the program as well as those who participated in it.

TABLE 5.3   Primary Questions in the Implementation Evaluation of the Child and Adolescent Trial for Cardiovascular Health

1. Participation—Did teachers, food service personnel, and PE specialists participate in the training sessions for the CATCH programs?
2. Dose—Were the components of the CATCH programs implemented?
3. Fidelity—Were the components of the CATCH programs implemented according to protocol?
4. Compatibility—Did the CATCH intervention programs fit the context of schools, as well as staff and teachers' needs, expectations, and values?

SOURCE: Adapted from Perry et al. (1997).

In CATCH, careful implementation evaluation was necessary because the program was being carried out simultaneously in California, Louisiana, Minnesota, and Texas, and it was important to be able to explain outcomes as well as the future feasibility of the program. In CATCH, we were concerned with four dimensions of implementation—participation, dose, fidelity, and compatibility. The primary questions that guided the implementation evaluation are shown in Table 5.3.

Careful data collection confirmed that CATCH was not only effective in changing eating and physical activity patterns, but it was feasible to implement in a large number of elementary schools in the United States (Perry et al., 1997). This was ascertained by documenting what percentage of people attended trainings, by direct observations of classrooms and physical education classes, by analyses of the food served at lunch, by written feedback from participants, and from school records.

The types of data that can be collected for implementation evaluation depend on the question being addressed, the targeted group, and budget considerations. Implementation evaluation can use existing records, self-report questionnaires, direct observations, interviews, or focus groups to obtain data and feedback on the health behavior program. There are excellent resources on program evaluation that provide considerable detail on each step in the design and conduct of implementation evaluation, including King et al.'s (1987) *How to Assess Program Implementation,* Patton's (1997) *Utilization-Focused Evaluation,* and Herman, Morris, and Fitz-Gibbon's (1987) *Evaluator's Handbook,* in addition to the references provided in Chapter 3 (where methods of obtaining information from the targeted groups was discussed).

An immediately useful outcome of implementation evaluation is to be able to improve implementation of an ongoing program. For example, classroom observations might reveal particular teachers or peer leaders who are having difficulty with the program and need additional, personalized training. Written reports from community organizers on their one-on-one interviews can reveal whether key issues are being discussed in these interviews, the sectors being reached, and how many are taking place so that guidance can be given to the organizer. Focus groups with those who are implementing a program can help to identify problems and potential solutions before the program is completed. When implementation evaluation is seen as helpful by the program's facilitators, they are much more receptive to data collection and observations and even welcome the opportunity to provide input into the implementation process.

Reports to the Community

It is important to provide timely reports to those involved in supporting and implementing the health behavior program. These can consist of reports on the behavior being targeted, implementation evaluation, outcomes, and recommendations. For example, in Project Northland, we produced an annual report from the student survey that documented tobacco, alcohol, and other drug use, as well as predictive factors and intervention exposure. Because the student surveys were conducted in the spring, we prepared a report that was delivered in early fall of the same year that summarized what had been learned from the student survey. The report was first sent to the school district, with a follow-up phone call for clarification. Then, a shorter report was prepared for use by the community staff for the community at large. This provided the schools and communities with an updated database for each year's efforts.

These reports are particularly important when changes are needed in a program, because they summarize the rationale for such changes. They are also critical if the program is to be maintained so that the positive effects of the program are widely shared and so that the program has a built-in system for improvement. The process of implementation evaluation and reporting should become part of the health behavior program so that ongoing improvements can be made, even if the original program developer is no longer involved with the program. Patton (1997) provides an excellent description of how reports can be prepared.

TABLE 5.4   Step 10: Maintaining Health Behavior Programs

The following questions provide the framework for determining how programs can be maintained:

1. What are the outcomes of the health behavior program? Were they robust and sufficient to warrant maintenance of the program?
2. Are there sufficient resources to maintain the program? Will the program have an ongoing champion? Are there sufficient people, money, time, collaborations, and sites?
3. Can the program be periodically updated based on ongoing implementation evaluation?

STEP 10: MAINTAINING
HEALTH BEHAVIOR PROGRAMS

The maintenance of successful community-wide health behavior programs is the goal of program development—to create a program that makes a difference over time in the lives of young people. Several questions provide the background for determining how health behavior programs can be maintained, as shown in Table 5.4.

The first consideration, then, is to decide if the health behavior program warrants maintenance. This can be determined from outcome and implementation evaluation data (Patton, 1997). Ideally, a health behavior program should have as an outcome at least short-term changes in young people's behavior to be considered successful. In our own work, we have not disseminated any of our programs until we have completed our studies, published our outcomes in scientific journals, and they have been positive. This means that some of our programs have ended up shelved, even after 2 or more years of program development work. Fortunately, these negative experiences eventually led to more powerful health behavior programs that were able to affect young people's behavior. A problem with maintaining a health behavior program that doesn't really work is that it often blocks the development of better, more comprehensive, and more powerful programs, because program resources are allocated, and the community has a sense of already doing something concerning that behavior. Therefore, it is better to recommend discontinuation of a program or to suggest improving the program before a final decision is made than to maintain a program that is not effective.

An exception might be if the health behavior program is just one component of a larger effort. For example, it may be that a program developer is asked to write a parent involvement program to supplement an ongoing drug education effort. The parent involvement program may not achieve behavior change as a single component, given the difficulty in reaching parents for health behavior change. However, if the implementation evaluation, for example, documents high parent participation, positive feedback from parents, and greater parent-child communication, and so forth, then it might be determined to be maintained, because it is a supplementary effort with positive intermediary outcomes. Again, the data collected to document participation, dose, fidelity, and compatibility can be useful in making a case that a given program should be maintained.

Before the decision to maintain a program can be made, an assessment of available resources should take place to make sure there are sufficient people, money, time, collaborations, and sites to continue the program. This is a similar analysis as was done prior to writing the health behavior program, as was discussed in Chapter 4. One additional resource would be the identification of a person who could be the so-called champion for the program (Smyth, 1997). This might be the program developer in some situations but more likely needs to be someone who has been part of the program in the schools or community. It seems particularly critical that a person be identified to stand behind, support, structure, and push for the program's maintenance within the community. Without this person, the needs of the program to be supported and consciously maintained can easily be overlooked.

The health behavior program will need to be updated on a regular basis, based on feedback from participants through observations, interviews, and implementation reports. Even the most creative and effective programs need updating and revisions, to better fit the mind-set of the targeted group and to accommodate secular trends. This can readily be seen with advertising, particularly for products aimed at young people. The themes of advertising reflect the current jargon and interests and styles of young people so that their products will be appealing enough for young people to purchase. Similarly, programs may need to update activities to be more relevant, examples to be more current, music to be more recent, and images to be more contemporary. In addition, activities or components that do not achieve ample participation may need to be revised to be more engaging to the participants or to the deliverer. This should be the ongoing work of the program developer along with the program's champion, to maintain a program that continues to be effective in changing the health behavior of young people.

SUMMARY OF THE TEN STEPS

In this book, 10 steps in program development have been discussed, along with examples from my work and others. There are numerous resources available for each of these steps that have been referenced throughout the book. These resources include other books, manuals, government reports, web sites, colleagues, creative people, and young people. The following (Table 5.5) provides a summary of each step and a checklist of what should be accomplished during each of the 10 steps.

The program developer who uses the steps described in this book should be able to create a health behavior program with a high likelihood that the program will affect the targeted behavior. However, as stated earlier in the book, not all of our programs have been successful. If behavior change is not accomplished, the mechanisms should be in place to strengthen the program, by reviewing the predictive factors selected (are they sufficiently potent?), the program components (were they powerful enough to change the predictive factors?), and program implementation (were all components of the program implemented as planned?). Table 5.6 provides a summary of the reasons why a program may not have achieved behavior change and next steps that can be taken to improve the outcomes of a program. By examining each of these reasons and how they may have manifested in developing the program, revisions can be made, and an updated, revised program can be tested.

ADDITIONAL CONSIDERATIONS

There are several issues and concerns that this book only touched on. The first is program design and evaluation, which is in itself the topic of numerous books, many of which were referenced throughout this book. Other issues and concerns are addressed in the following discussion.

TABLE 5.5   Checklist of the Steps in Program Development

Steps	What Should Be Accomplished?
1. Selecting health behaviors	The health behavior(s) to be targeted should be identified.
2. Providing a rationale	A summary of the consequences and epidemiology of the behavior is written, as well as a list of the major predictive environmental, personal, and behavioral factors.
3. Creating an intervention model	The intervention model is created with the targeted group, outcome behavior(s), and most potent predictive factors specified.
4. Writing intervention objectives	The intervention objectives are written from the predictive factors and should be feasible and potentially potent.
5. Applying intervention objectives	Data are gathered to ensure that the intervention objectives are compatible with the mind-set of the targeted group(s) and community.
6. Reviewing types of programs	A summary grid is developed of prior intervention programs or program components that would be appropriate for each intervention objective.
7. Creating program components	Using prior programs and new ideas from a creative team, a prioritized list of program components is written that will address each intervention objective across the types of programs selected.
8. Constructing the program	After determining resources and an overall motif, the program is written or produced, packaged, and piloted with the targeted group(s).
9. Implementing the program	The health behavior program is introduced to key people for support and implementation, training is undertaken, the program takes place, implementation evaluation is conducted, and feedback provided to the community.
10. Maintaining the program	If the health behavior program is successful, then resources are assessed and a champion identified, to determine how the program will be maintained.

Multiple Behaviors

Many of the health behaviors of young people are correlated, such as the use of tobacco and alcohol (USDHHS, 1994). Moreover, some have a

TABLE 5.6 Potential Reasons for an Unsuccessful Health Behavior Program and Next Steps to Improve the Program

Reason	Description	Next Steps
1. Model or theory problems	The wrong predictors were selected; they did not account for a large enough explanation of the behavior.	Reexamine the predictors and add or replace more potent predictors to the intervention model.
2. Intervention problems	The intervention was not powerful enough to modify the predictive factors; the intervention may not have fit the mind-set of the targeted group. Potent macro-level influences, such as cultural norms, were not affected by the intervention.	Create new program components and conduct extensive focus groups and a pilot study to examine the potency of these new components.
3. Implementation problems	The health behavior program was not implemented as planned; the program was not conducted by the facilitators as was expected or there was a lack of attendance and participation. The community may not have been ready for or supportive of the program.	Conduct meetings with community representatives to ensure their commitment. Lengthen the training sessions so there is adequate time for rehearsal and planning. Observe the health behavior program while it is being implemented.
4. Evaluation problems	The evaluation did not measure the actual effects of the program; there may have been inadequate survey instruments, low participation, or contamination with control groups.	Discuss discrepancies between observed and measured outcomes. Develop new instruments. Conduct meetings with community members to improve participation and stem contamination.

similar etiology, with similar predictive factors (Jessor & Jessor, 1977). The question that emerges is whether health behavior programs should be developed to address multiple, related behaviors at the same time. The experience of our research suggests that the answer to this is both "no" and "yes." Behaviors such as smoking, alcohol, and marijuana use do have a similar etiology and predictive factors. However, they are often perceived uniquely by young people so that the context of these behaviors is not necessarily similar. In the Class of 1989 Study, smoking, alcohol, and marijuana use were addressed in the behavioral health curriculum in the ninth grade. However, the larger Minnesota Heart Health Program did not have messages concerning alcohol or marijuana use. We observed short-term changes in alcohol and marijuana use at the end of ninth grade but longer-term changes in cigarette use (Perry et al., 1994a). The added community component was necessary to provide enough behavioral strength to maintain the change in cigarette use.

We did observe changes in multiple behaviors in the Class of 1989 Study and CATCH. In the Class of 1989 Study, behavioral health curricula were devoted to nutrition, smoking, and physical activity in the sixth through eighth grades, respectively (Perry, Klepp, et al., 1989). In CATCH, nutrition and physical activity were presented in the third through fifth grades and smoking prevention in the fifth grade. Therefore, it seems that "yes," multiple behaviors can be included in a given health behavior program, *if* sufficient time and attention is devoted to each behavior within the program. The steps described in this book can be followed for two or more behaviors, with the work done separately for each behavior, until Steps 7 or 8, when the program is conceptualized, written, and produced. The key is to have program components that address each intervention objective for each behavior.

Community Involvement

This book assumes that a behavior has been or will be selected by a group, organization, school, or community, and a health behavior program is developed to address changes in that behavior. There has been quite a lot of discussion concerning who should make the decision about which behaviors are to be included in a community-wide program, because government mandates or outside funding sources may not represent the needs of a given community. This book does not really address this issue. Even the community action programs described are oriented toward changes in a given health behavior. The steps outlined in this book are really independent of how the targeted health behavior has been chosen, with the recognition that many programs are mandated (and should be developed to be as successful as possible) and that those that are decided by community members may result in better implementation (Gielen & McDonald, 1997).

For example, in a study in which stakeholders—a task force of school, community members, students, parents—decided on the content of a nutrition program, rather than the researchers, the stakeholders decided that they wanted a classroom program that would change students' eating patterns (Harvey, Spillman, & Perry, 1996). The researchers were asked to develop such a program. Even though they began with a bottom-up model of decision making, the researchers found that they were still asked to develop a health behavior program and so still needed to follow the steps outlined earlier.

Another challenge emerges when the community wants to focus on larger sociodemographic changes, such as issues of poverty and housing. This focus is not incompatible with the steps outlined, particularly if the outcomes desired can be articulated in behavioral terms, such as "each student will eat a balanced and nutritious meal at school." These larger issues can also benefit by thinking in terms of a range of program components that might affect outcomes and specifically, by using community organization methods that have been successful in other programs. The careful specification of outcomes, the provision of a cohesive rationale, the centrality of etiologic and predictive factors, and the review of prior efforts are all important steps in being able to understand a problem and the types of available solutions.

Orientation of a Health Behavior Program

Although health behavior programs have been labeled as programs that blame the victim, the steps outlined in this book stress the importance of environmental factors in the etiology of young people's behavior. Community-wide programs can address many levels of the social environment, but they have limited power to affect exposure to mass media images, role models, and messages, which significantly influence young people's behavior (Perry, 1998). Therefore, in addition to community-wide efforts, program developers should consider their professional roles as including support and action for changes in the larger cultural conditions that influence children, such as the policies and practices that affect young people's exposure to mass media, advertising, and promotional activities, as well as social policies that affect their overall well-being.

Health professionals can also lobby for more overall financial support for promoting the health of young people. The programs described in Chapter 1 were supported by research grants or foundation monies that made their scale and scope possible. The replication of these programs (and others) is often not given ample support. An example of what is needed in terms of support is provided by cigarette smoking. During the Fairness Doctrine era (1967-1971), 1 antismoking advertisement was mandated to be shown on television for every 12 prosmoking advertisements. The result was a decrease in teen smoking at a time when the rates of teen smoking had been increasing (USDHHS, 1994). The decrease was particularly notable during the first year of the Fairness Doctrine era. This provides a clue as to the resources needed to counter messages that promote health-compromising behaviors. Thus, if the tobacco industry devotes $6 billion a year to tobacco advertising and promotional activities in the United States, it stands to reason that about $1 billion should be devoted just to antismoking counteradvertising. Other behaviors—alcohol use, high-fat food consumption, and so on—are supported through advertising and promotional activities. A society that allows such extensive promotion of health-compromising behaviors might also increase the promotion of healthy lifestyles as well. Greater overall support for the health and well-being of youths in our society is clearly needed and warranted.

A FINAL WORD

I've been asked which steps have been most important in the development of our successful health behavior programs. First, using behavioral theories as the basis for intervention objectives has served to create an umbrella under which more powerful and appropriate behavioral programs could continually be developed. The second has been the creative team approach, of meeting and working with creative people to develop programs that were fun, humorous, engaging, attractive, and interesting, in addition to being effective. Learning to be healthy should be a positive experience for young people, especially when so many health-compromising activities crowd the media and are portrayed as what is meant by "having fun." The third has been the feedback, input, and collaboration of the targeted groups—generally, teens, parents, and community members—as they welcome new approaches to solving problems and take the risk of applying these new approaches in their schools, homes, and communities.

Last, the very first step—choosing a health behavior—is perhaps most critical. The choice of the behavior drives the process, so it is important that the behavior be considered carefully. In particular, the behavior needs to be viewed from the perspective of the young person. The behavior may be functional from his or her perspective, and health-enhancing alternatives may be needed. The behavior most likely affects physical, psychological, social, and spiritual health, so it is important that changes in behavior enhance or serve to balance those domains. The choice of the behavior and the commitment of a community to improve the health of young people signifies the level of caring of the community for its young. Thus, this commitment is a way to begin to address how to create the village it takes to raise our children.

REFERENCES

Allensworth, D., & Kolbe, L. J. (1987). The comprehensive school health program: Exploring an expanded concept. *Journal of School Health, 57,* 409-412.

Andrews, D. W., Soberman, L. H., & Dishion, T. J. (1995). The Adolescent Transitions Program for high-risk teens and their parents: Toward a school-based intervention. *Education and Treatment of Children, 18,* 478-498.

Arkin, R. M., Roemhild, H. F., Johnson, C. A., Luepker, R. V., & Murray, D. M. (1981). The Minnesota smoking prevention program: A seventh grade health curriculum supplement. *Journal of School Health, 51,* 611-616.

Bandura, A. (1977). *Social learning theory.* Englewood Cliffs, NJ: Prentice Hall.

Bandura, A. (1986). *Social foundations of thought and action: A social cognitive theory.* Englewood Cliffs, NJ: Prentice Hall.

Bandura, A. (1995). *Self-efficacy in changing societies.* New York: Cambridge University Press.

Baranowski, T., & Nader, P. R. (1985). Family health behavior. In D. C. Turk & R. D. Kerns (Eds.), *Health, illness, and families: A life-span perspective* (pp. 51-80). New York: Wiley-Interscience.

Baranowski, T., Perry, C. L., & Parcel, G. S. (1997). How individuals, environments, and health behavior interact: Social cognitive theory. In K. Glanz, F. M. Lewis, & B. K. Rimer (Eds.), *Health behavior and health education: Theory, research, and practice, 2nd edition* (pp. 153-178). San Francisco: Jossey-Bass.

Bauman, K. E., & Fisher, L. A. (1985). Subjective expected utility, locus of control, and behavior. *Journal of Applied Social Psychology, 15,* 606-621.

Bell, R. M., Ellickson, P. L., & Harrison, E. R. (1993). Do drug prevention effects persist into high school? How Project ALERT did with ninth graders. *Preventive Medicine, 22,* 463-483.

Black, D. R., Tobler N. S., & Sciacca, J. P. (1998). Peer helping/involvement: An efficacious way to meet the challenge of reducing alcohol, tobacco, and other drug use among youth? *Journal of School Health, 68,* 87-93.

Blackburn, H., Luepker, R. V., Kline, F. G., Bracht, N., Carlaw, R., Jacobs, D., Mittelmark, M., Stauffer, L., & Taylor, H. L. (1984). The Minnesota Heart Health Program: A research and demonstration project in cardiovascular disease prevention. In J. D. Matarazzo, S. M. Weiss, J. A. Herd, N. E. Miller, & S. M. Weiss (Eds.), *Behavioral health: A handbook of health enhancement and disease prevention* (pp. 1171-1178). New York: John Wiley.

Blaine, T. M., Forster, J. L., Hennrikus, D., O'Neil, S., Wolfson, M., & Pham, H. (1997). Creating tobacco policy control at the local level: Implementation of a direct action organizing approach. *Health Education and Behavior, 24,* 640-651.

Blum, R. W., & Stark, T. (1985). Cognitive development in adolescence: Clinical cues and implication. *Seminars in Adolescent Medicine, 1,* 25-32.

Botvin, G. J., Baker, E., Renick, N. L., Filazzola, A. D., & Botvin, E. M. (1984). A cognitive-behavioral approach to substance abuse prevention. *Addictive Behaviors, 9,* 137-147.

Botvin, G. J., Baker, E., Dusenbury, L., Botvin, E. M., & Diaz, T. (1995). Long-term follow-up results of a randomized drug abuse prevention trial in a white middle-class population. *Journal of the American Medical Association, 273,* 1106-1112.

Bracht, N. (Ed.). (1990). *Health promotion at the community level.* Newbury Park, CA: Sage.

Bracht, N. (Ed.). (1999). *Health promotion at the community level* (2nd ed., rev.). Thousand Oaks, CA: Sage.

Breslow, L. (1990). Foreword. In N. Bracht (Ed.), *Health promotion at the community level.* Newbury Park, CA: Sage.

Caballero, B., Davis, S., Davis, C. E., Ethelbah, B., Evans, M., Lohman, T., Stephenson, L., Story, M., & White, J. (in press). Pathways: A school-based program for the primary prevention of obesity in American Indian children. *Journal of Nutritional Biochemistry.*

Carnegie Council on Adolescent Development. (1992). *A matter of time: Risk and opportunity in the nonschool hours.* New York: Carnegie Corporation.

Centers for Disease Control and Prevention. (1988). Guidelines for effective school health education to prevent the spread of AIDS. *Morbidity and Mortality Weekly Report, 37,* 1-14.

Centers for Disease Control and Prevention. (1994). Guidelines for school health programs to prevent tobacco use and addiction. *Morbidity and Mortality Weekly Report, 43,* 1-18.

Centers for Disease Control and Prevention. (1996a). Guidelines for school health programs to promote healthy eating. *Morbidity and Mortality Weekly Report, 45,* 1-41.

Centers for Disease Control and Prevention. (1996b). Projected smoking-related deaths among youth—United States. *Morbidity and Mortality Weekly Report, 45,* 971-974.

Centers for Disease Control and Prevention. (1997). Guidelines for school and community programs to promote lifelong physical activity among young people. *Journal of School Health, 67,* 202-219.

Chassin, L., Presson, C. C., & Sherman, S. J. (1990). Social psychological contributions to the understanding and prevention of adolescent cigarette smoking. *Personality and Social Psychology, 16,* 133-151.

Collins, J. L., Small, M. L., Kann, L., Pateman, B. C., Gold, R. S., & Kolbe, L. J. (1995). School health education. *Journal of School Health, 65,* 302-311.

Conrad, K. M., Flay, B. R., & Hill, D. (1992). Why children start smoking cigarettes: Predictors of onset. *British Journal of Addiction, 87,* 1711-1724.

Contento, I., Balch, G. I., Bronner, Y. L., Lytle, L. A., Maloney, S. K., Olson, C. M., & Swadener, S. S. (1995). The effectiveness of nutrition education and implications for nutrition education policy, programs, and research: A review of research. *Journal of Nutrition Education, 27,* 284-418.

Creswell, J. W. (1994). *Research design: Qualitative and quantitative approaches.* Thousand Oaks, CA: Sage.

Crockett, L. J., & Petersen, A. C. (1993). Adolescent development: Health risks and opportunities for health promotion. In S. G. Millstein, A. C. Petersen, & E. O. Nightingale (Eds.), *Promoting the health of adolescents* (pp. 13-37). New York: Oxford University Press.

Cullen, K. W., Bartholomew, L. K., Parcel, G. S., & Kok, G. (1998). Intervention mapping: Use of theory and data in the development of a fruit and vegetable nutrition program for Girl Scouts. *Journal of Nutrition Education, 30,* 188-195.

Depression Guideline Panel. (1993). *Depression in primary care: Volume 1.* Rockville, MD: USDHHS.

DiClemente, R. J., Hansen, W. B., & Ponton, L. J. (Eds.). (1996). *Handbook of adolescent health risk behavior.* New York: Plenum.

Dishion, T. J., & Andrews, D. W. (1995). Preventing escalation in problem behaviors with high-risk young adolescents: Immediate and 1-year outcomes. *Journal of Consulting and Clinical Psychology, 63,* 538-548.

Drug Strategies. (1996). *Making the grade: A guide to school drug prevention programs.* Washington, DC: Author.

Drug Strategies. (1998). *Safe schools, safe students: A guide to violence prevention strategies.* Washington, DC: Author.

Dryfoos, J. G. (1994). *Full-service schools.* San Francisco: Jossey-Bass.

Dryfoos, J. G. (1998). *Safe passage: Making it through adolescence in a risky society.* New York: Oxford University Press.

Dusenbury, L., & Falco, M. (1995). Eleven components of effective drug abuse prevention curricula. *Journal of School Health, 65,* 420-425.

Edmundson, E., Parcel, G. S., Feldman, H. A., Elder, J., Perry, C. L., Johnson, C. C., Williston, B. J., Stone, E., Yang, M., Lytle, L., & Webber, L. (1996). The effects of the Child and Adolescent Trial for Cardiovascular Health upon psychosocial determinants of diet and physical activity behavior. *Preventive Medicine, 25,* 442-454.

Elder, J. P., Perry, C. L., Stone, E. J., Johnson, C. C., Yang, M., Edmundson, E. W., Smyth, M. H., Galati, T., Feldman, H., Cribb, P., & Parcel, G. S. (1996). Tobacco use measurement, prediction and intervention in elementary schools in four states: The CATCH study. *Preventive Medicine, 25,* 486-494.

Ellison, R. C., Capper, A. L., Goldberg, R. J., Witschi, J. C., & Stare, F. C. (1989). The environmental component: Changing food service to promote cardiovascular health. *Health Education Quarterly, 16,* 285-297.

Epstein, L. H., & Wing, R. R. (1987). Behavioral treatment of childhood obesity. *Psychological Bulletin, 101,* 331-342.

Fishbein, M., & Ajzen, I. (1975). *Belief, attitude, intention and behavior: An introduction to theory and research.* Reading, MA: Addison-Wesley.

Fitzpatrick, M. P., Chapman, G. E., & Barr, S. I. (1997). Lower-fat menu items in restaurants satisfy customers. *Journal of the American Dietetic Association, 97,* 510-514.

Flores, R. (1995). Dance for health—Improving fitness in African American and Hispanic adolescents. *Public Health Reports, 110,* 189-193.

Food Marketing Institute. (1987). *Trends, 1987: Consumer attitudes and the supermarket.* Washington, DC: Author.

Forster, J. L. (1982). A communitarian ethical model for public health interventions: An alternative to individual behavior change strategies. *Journal of Public Health Policy, 3,* 150-163.

Forster, J. L., McGovern, P. G., Wagenaar, A. C., Wolfson, M., Perry, C. L., & Anstine, P. S. (1994). The ability of young people to purchase alcohol without age identification. *Addiction, 89,* 699-705.

Forster, J. L., Wolfson, M., Murray, D. M., Blaine, T. M., Wagenaar, A. C., & Hennrikus, D. J. (1998). The effects of community policies to reduce youth access to tobacco. *American Journal of Public Health, 88,* 1193-1196.

Gielen, A. C., & McDonald, E. M. (1997). The Precede-Proceed planning model. In K. Glanz, F. M. Lewis, & B. K. Rimer (Eds.), *Health education and health behavior: Theory, research and practice* (pp. 359-383). San Francisco: Jossey-Bass.

Gittelsohn, J., Evans, M., Helitzer, D., Anliker, J., Story, M., Metcalfe, L., Davis, S., & Iron Cloud, P. (1998). Formative research in a school-based obesity prevention program for Native American school children (Pathways). *Health Education Research, 13,* 251-265.

Glanz, K., Lankenau, B., Foerster, S., Temple, S., Mullis, R., & Schmid, T. (1995). Environmental and policy approaches to cardiovascular disease prevention through nutrition —Opportunities for state and local action. *Health Education Quarterly, 22,* 512-527.

Glanz, K., Lewis, F. M., & Rimer, B. K. (Eds.). (1997). *Health education and health behavior: Theory research and practice* (2nd ed.). San Francisco: Jossey-Bass.

Hansen, W. B. (1992). School-based substance abuse prevention: A review of the state of the art in curriculum, 1980-1990. *Health Education Research, 7,* 403-430.

Hansen, W. B., & Graham, J. W. (1991). Preventing alcohol, marijuana, and cigarette use among adolescents: Peer pressure resistance training versus establishing conservative norms. *Preventive Medicine, 20,* 414-430.

Hansen, W. B., Graham, J. W., Sobel, J. L., Shelton, D. R., Flay, B. R., & Johnson, C. A. (1987). The consistency of peer and parent influences on tobacco, alcohol, and marijuana use among young adolescents. *Journal of Behavioral Medicine, 10,* 559-579.

Harvey, P. W. J., Spillman, D. A., & Perry, C. L. (1996). Stakeholder participation in the development of a nutrition education program at an Australian secondary school. *Health Promotion Journal of Australia, 6,* 21-27.

Hochbaum, G. M., Sorenson, J. R., & Lorig, K. (1992). Theory in health education practice. *Health Education Quarterly, 19,* 295-313.

Heaney, C. A., & Israel, B. A. (1997). Social networks and social support. In K. Glanz, F. M. Lewis, & B. K. Rimer (Eds.), *Health education and health behavior: Theory, research and practice* (pp. 179-205). San Francisco: Jossey-Bass.

Henriksen, E. M. (1991). A peer helping program for the middle school. *Canadian Journal of Counseling, 25,* 12-18.

Herman, J. L., Morris, L. L., & Fitz-Gibbon, C. T. (1987). *An evaluator's handbook.* Newbury Park: Sage.

Hill, J. P., & Holmbeck, G. N. (1986). Attachment and autonomy during adolescence. *Annals of Child Development, 3,* 145-189.

Jessor, R., & Jessor, S. L. (1977). *Problem behavior and psychosocial development: A longitudinal study of youth.* New York: Academic Press.

Johnson, C.C., Osganian, S. K., Budman, S. B., Lytle, L. A., Barrera, E. P., Bonura, S. R., Wu, M. C., & Nader, P. R. (1994). CATCH: Family process evaluation of a multicenter trial. *Health Education Quarterly, Supplement 2,* 91-106.

Johnson, D. W., Johnson, R. T., & Dudley, B. (1992). Effects of peer mediation on elementary school students. *Mediation Quarterly, 10,* 89-99.

Johnston, L. D., O'Malley, P. M., & Bachman, J. G. (1996). *National survey results on drug use from the Monitoring the Future study, 1975-1995. Secondary school students.* Washington DC: USDHHS.

Kann, L., Collins, J. L., Pateman, B. C., Small, M. L., Russ, J. G., & Kolbe, L. J. (1995). The School Health Policies and Programs Study (SHPPS): Rationale for a nationwide status report on school health programs. *Journal of School Health, 65,* 291-294.

Kann, L, Kolbe, L. J., & Collins, J. L. (Eds.). (1993). Measuring the health behavior of adolescents: The Youth Risk Behavior Surveillance System and recent reports on high-risk adolescents. *Public Health Reports, 108,* 1-67.

Kelder, S. H., Perry, C. L., & Klepp, K-I. (1993). Communitywide youth exercise education: Long-term outcomes of the Minnesota Heart Health Program. *Journal of School Health, 63,* 218-223.

Kelder, S. H., Perry, C. L., Klepp, K-I., & Lytle, L. A. (1994). Longitudinal tracking of adolescent smoking physical activity, and food choice behaviors. *American Journal of Public Health, 84,* 1121-1126.

Kelder, S. H., Perry, C. L., Lytle, L. L., & Klepp. K-I. (1993). Community-wide youth nutrition education: Long-term outcomes of the Minnesota Heart Health Program and the Class of 1989 Study, *Journal of School Health, 63,* 218-223.

Kim, S., McLeod, J. H., Rader, D., & Johnston, G. (1992). An evaluation of a prototype school-based peer counseling program. *Journal of Drug Education, 22,* 37-53.

King, J. A., Morris L. L., & Fitz-Gibbon, C. T. (1987). *How to assess program implementation.* Newbury Park: Sage.

Kinston, W., Loader P., & Miller, L. (1988). Talking to families about obesity: A controlled study. *International Journal of Eating Disorders, 7,* 261-275.

Kledges, R. C., Coates, T. J., Brown, G., Sturgeon-Tillisch, J., Moldenhauer-Kledges, L. M., Holzer, B., Woolfrey, J., & Vollmer, J. (1983). Parental influences on children's eating behavior and relative weight. *Journal of Applied Behavioral Analysis, 16,* 371-378.

Klepp, K-I., Halper, A., & Perry, C. L. (1986). The efficacy of peer leaders in drug abuse prevention. *Journal of School Health, 56,* 407-411.

Klepp, K-I., Kelder, S. H., & Perry, C. L. (April, 1994). *Do peer leaders in youth health promotion programs benefit from their teaching experiences?* Poster presented at the Society of Behavioral Medicine, Boston.

Klepp, K-I., Kelder, S. H., & Perry, C. L. (1995). Alcohol and marijuana use among adolescents: Long-term outcomes of the Class of 1989 Study. *Annals of Behavioral Medicine, 17,* 19-24.

Klepp, K-I., Perry, C. L., Hawkins, K. (1985). The Health Olympics: Intervention challenges by adolescent for adolescents. *The ACHPER National Journal, 5-6,* 1985.

Kolbe, L. (1990). An epidemiological surveillance system to monitor the prevalence of youth behaviors that most affect health. *Journal of Health Education, 21,* 44-48.

Komro, K. A., Hu, F. B., & Flay, B. R. (1997). A public health perspective on urban adolescents. In H. J. Walberg, O. Reyes, & R. P. Weissberg (Eds.), *Children and youth: Interdisciplinary perspectives, Vol. 7* (pp. 253-298). Thousand Oaks, CA: Sage.

Komro, K. A., Perry, C. L., Murray, D. M., Veblen-Mortenson, S., Williams, C. L., & Anstine, P. S. (1996). Peer planned social activities for the prevention of alcohol use among young adolescents. *Journal of School Health, 66,* 328-333.

Komro, K. A., Perry, C. L., Veblen-Mortenson, S., & Williams, C. L. (1994). Peer participation in Project Northland: A community-wide alcohol use prevention project. *Journal of School Health, 64,* 318-322.

Komro, K. A., Perry, C. L., Veblen-Mortenson, S., Williams, C. L., & Roel, J. P. (in press). Peer leadership in school and community alcohol use prevention activities. *Journal of Health Education.*

Komro, K. A., Perry, C. L., Williams, C. L., Veblen-Mortenson, S., Forster, J. L., Munson, K. A., Farbakhsh, K., Lachter, R. B., & Pratt, L. K. (in press). Research and evaluation design of a community-wide program to reduce adolescent alcohol use: Phase II of Project

Northland. In *Community action research and the prevention of alcohol and other drug problems*. Wellington, New Zealand: Alcoholic Advisory Council.

Kroehnert, G. (1995). *Basic training for trainers* (2nd ed.). Sydney, Australia: McGraw-Hill.

Krueger, R. A. (1988). *Focus groups: A practical guide for applied research*. Newbury Park, CA: Sage

Kvale, S. (1996). *Interviews: An introduction to qualitative research interviewing*. Thousand Oaks, CA: Sage.

Luepker, R. V., Murray, D. M., Jacobs, D. R., Mittelmark, M. B., Bracht, N., Carlaw, R., Crow, R., Elmer, P., Finnegan, J., Folsom, A. R., Grimm, R., Hannan, P. J., Jeffery, R., Lando, H., McGovern, P., Mullis, R., Perry, C. L., Pechacek, T., Pirie, P., Sprafka, M., Weisbrod, R., & Blackburn, H. (1994). Community education for cardiovascular disease prevention: Risk factor changes in the Minnesota Heart Health Program. *American Journal of Public Health, 84,* 1383-1393.

Luepker, R. V., Perry, C. L., McKinlay, S. M., Nader, P. R., Parcel, G. S., Stone, E. J., Webber, L. S., Elder, J. P., Feldman, H. A., Johnson, C. C., Kelder, S. H., & Wu, M. (1996). Outcomes of a field trial to improve children's dietary patterns and physical activity: The Child and Adolescent Trial for Cardiovascular Health (CATCH). *Journal of the American Medical Association, 275,* 768-776.

Lytle, L. A., Kelder, S. H., Perry, C. L., & Klepp, K-I. (1995). Covariance of adolescent health behaviors: The Class of 1989 Study. *Health Education Research, 10,* 133-146.

Lytle, L. A., Kelder S. H., & Snyder, M. P. (1992). A review of school food service research. *School Food Service Research Review, 16,* 7-13.

Lytle, L. A., & Roski, J. (1997). Unhealthy eating and other risk-taking behavior: Are they related? *Annals of the New York Academy of Sciences, 817,* 49-65.

Lytle, L. A., Stone, E. J., Nichaman, M. Z., Perry, C. L., Montgomery, D. H., Nicklas, T. A., Zive, M. M., Mitchell, P., Dwyer, J. T., Ebzery, M. K., Evans, M. A., & Galati, T. P. (1996). Changes in nutrient intakes of elementary school children following a school-based intervention: Results from the CATCH study. *Preventive Medicine, 25,* 65-477.

McAlister, A., Perry, C. L., & Maccoby, N. (1979). Adolescent smoking: Onset and prevention. *Pediatrics, 63,* 650-658.

McAlister, A., Perry, C. L., Killen, J., Slinkard, L., & Maccoby, N. (1980). Pilot study of smoking, alcohol and drug abuse prevention. *American Journal of Public Health, 70,* 719-721.

McKenzie, T. L., Nader, P. R., Strikmiller, P. K., Yang, M., Stone, E. J., Perry, C. L., Taylor, W. C., Epping, J. N., Feldman, H. A., Luepker, R. V., & Kelder, S. H. (1996). School physical education: Effects of the Child and Adolescent Trial for Cardiovascular Health. *Preventive Medicine, 25,* 423-431.

Mittelmark, M. B., Luepker, R. V., Jacobs, D., Bracht, N.F., Carlaw, R., Crow, R., Finnegan, J., Grimm, R. H., Jeffery, R. W., Kline, F. G., Murray, D. M., Mullis, R., Perry, C., Pirie, P., Pechacek,T. F., & Blackburn, H. (1986). The Minnesota Heart Health program's community-wide education strategy: The Mankato experience. *Preventive Medicine, 15,* 1-17.

Montano, D. E., Kasprzyk, D., & Taplin, S. H. (1997). The theory of reasoned action and the theory of planned behavior. In K. Glanz, F. M. Lewis, & B. K. Rimer (Eds.), *Health education and health behavior: Theory, research and practice* (pp. 85-112). San Francisco: Jossey-Bass.

Montgomery, L. E., Kiely, J. L., & Pappas, G. (1996). The effects of poverty, race, and family structure on US children's health: Data from the NHIS, 1978 through 1980 and 1989 through 1991. *American Journal of Public Health, 86,* 1401-1405.

Morgaine, C. A. (1992). Alternative paradigms for helping families change themselves. *Family Relations, 41,* 12-17.

Morgan, D. L., & Krueger, R. A. (1998). *The focus group kit.* Thousand Oaks, CA: Sage.

Moscicki, E. V. (1995). Epidemiology of suicidal behavior. *Suicide and Life-Threatening Behavior,* 25, 22-35.

Murray, D. M. (1998). *Design and analysis of group-randomized trials.* New York: Oxford University Press.

Murray, D. M., Perry, C. L., Griffin, G., Harty, K. C., Jacobs, D. R., Schmid, L., Daly, K., & Pallonen, U. (1992). Results from a statewide approach to adolescent tobacco use prevention. *Preventive Medicine, 21,* 449-472.

Murray, D. M., Pirie, P., Luepker, R. V., & Pallonen, U. (1989). Five- and six-year follow-up results from four seventh-grade smoking prevention strategies. *Journal of Behavioral Medicine, 12,* 207-218.

Nader, P. R., Baranowski, R., Vanderpool, N. A., Dunn, K., Dworkin, R., & Ray, L. (1983). The family health project: Cardiovascular risk reduction education for children and parents. *Developmental and Behavioral Pediatrics, 4,* 3-9.

Nader, P. R., Sallis, J. F., Abramson, I. S., Broyles, S. L., Patterson, T. L., Senn, K., Rupp, J.W., & Nelson, J. A. (1992). Family-based cardiovascular risk reduction education among Mexican- and Anglo-Americans. *Family and Community Health, 15,* 57-74.

Nader, P. R., Sallis, J. F., Patterson, T. L., Abramson, I. S., Rupp, J. W., Senn, K. L., Atkins, C. J., Roppe, B. E., Morris, J. A., Wallace, J. P., & Vega, W. A. (1989). A family approach to cardiovascular risk reduction: Results from the San Diego Family Health Project. *Health Education Quarterly, 16,* 229-244.

Nader, P. R., Sellers, D. E., Johnson, C. C., Perry, C. L., Stone, E. J., Cook, K. C., Bebechuk, J., & Luepker, R. V. (1996). The effect of adult participation in a school-based family intervention to improve children's diet and physical activity: The Child and Adolescent Trial for Cardiovascular Health. *Preventive Medicine, 25,* 455-464.

Nader, P. R., Stone, E. J., Lytle, L. A., Perry, C. L., Osganian, V., Kelder, S. H., Webber, L., Elder, J., Montgomery, D., Feldman, H., Wu, M., Johnson, C., Parcel, G., & Luepker, R. V. (in press). Three-year maintenance of improved diet and physical activities: The CATCH cohort. *Archives of Pediatrics & Adolescent Medicine.*

National Peer Helpers Association. (1990). Programmatic standards. *Peer Facilitators Quarterly, 4,* 8-12.

Nichols, L. A. S., & Schmidt, M. K. (1995). The impact of videotapes in educating grocery store shoppers about fat and cholesterol. *Journal of Nutrition Education, 27,* 5-10.

Nutbeam, D. (1997). Promoting health and preventing disease: An international perspective on youth health promotion. *Journal of Adolescent Health, 20,* 396-402.

Nutbeam, D., & Harris, E. (1998). *Theory in a nutshell: A practitioner's guide to commonly used theories and models in health promotion.* Sydney, Australia: University of Sydney, National Centre for Health Promotion.

Ozer, E. M., Brindis, C. D., Millstein, S. G., Knopt, D. K., & Irwin, C. E. (1997). *America's adolescents: Are they healthy?* San Francisco: University of California, San Francisco, School of Medicine, National Adolescent Health Information Center.

Parcel, G. S., Eriksen, M. P., Lovato, C. Y., Gottlieb, N. H., & Brink, S. G. (1989). The diffusion of school-based tobacco-use prevention programs: Project description and baseline data. *Health Education Research, 4,* 111-124.

Patterson, T., Sallis, J., Nader, P., Rupp, J., McKenzie, T., Roppe, B., & Bartok, P. (1988). Direct observation of physical activity and dietary behaviors in a structured environment: Effects of a family-based health promotion program. *Journal of Behavioral Medicine, 11,* 447-458.

Patton, M. Q. (1997). *Utilization-focused evaluation* (3rd ed.). Thousand Oaks, CA: Sage.

Pentz, M. A., Dwyer, J. H., MacKinnon, D. P., Flay, B. R., Hansen, W. B., Wang, E. Y., & Johnson, C. A. (1989). A multicommunity trial for primary prevention of adolescent drug abuse. *Journal of the American Medical Association, 261,* 3259-3266.

Perry, C. L. (1986). Community-wide health promotion and drug abuse prevention. *Journal of School Health, 56,* 359-363.

Perry, C. L. (1998). The relationship between "Share of Voice" and "Share of Market" and implications for youth health promotion. *Journal of Health Education, 29,* 206-212.

Perry, C. L., Baranowski, T., & Parcel, G. (1990). How individuals, environments, and health behavior interact: Social learning theory. In K. Glanz, F. M. Lewis, & B. Rimer, (Eds.), *Health behavior and health education: Theory, research, and practice.* San Francisco: Jossey-Bass.

Perry, C. L., Bishop, D. B., Taylor, G., Murray, D. M., Mays, R. W., Dudovitz, B. S., Smyth, M., & Story, M. (1998). Changing fruit and vegetable consumption among children: The 5-A-Day Power Plus Program in Saint Paul, Minnesota. *American Journal of Public Health, 88,* 603-609

Perry, C. L., & Grant, M. (1991). A cross-cultural pilot study on alcohol education and young people. *World Health Statistics Quarterly, 44,* 70-73.

Perry, C. L., Grant, M., Ernberg, G., Florenzano, R. U., Langdon, M. D., Blaze-Temple, D., Cross, D., Jacobs, D. R., Myeni, A. D., Waahlberg, R. B., Berg, S., Andersson, D., Fisher, K. J., Saunders, B., & Schmid, T. (1989). W.H.O. collaborative study on alcohol education and young people: Outcomes of a four-country pilot study. *International Journal of Addictions, 24,* 1145-1171.

Perry, C. L., & Jessor, R. (1985). The concept of health promotion and the prevention of adolescent drug abuse. *Health Education Quarterly, 12,* 169-184.

Perry, C. L., & Kelder, S. H. (1993). Substance abuse: Smoking, alcohol and drugs. In D. Glenwick & L. Jason (Eds.), *Promoting health and mental health in children, youth, and families.* New York: Springer.

Perry, C. L., Kelder, S. H., & Klepp, K-I. (1994a). Communitywide cardiovascular disease prevention with young people: Long-term outcomes of the Class of 1989 Study. *European Journal of Public Health, 4,* 188-194.

Perry, C. L., Kelder, S. H., & Klepp, K-I. (1994b). The rationale behind early prevention of cardiovascular disease with young people. *European Journal of Public Health, 4,* 156-162.

Perry, C. L., Kelder, S. H., & Komro, K. (1993). The social world of adolescents: Family, peers, schools, and community. In S. G. Millstein, A. C. Petersen, & E. O. Nightingale (Eds.), *Promoting the health of adolescents: New directions for the twenty-first century* (pp. 73-95). New York: Oxford University Press.

Perry, C. L., Kelder, S. H., Murray, D. M., & Klepp, K-I. (1992). Community-wide smoking prevention: Long-term outcomes of the Minnesota Heart Health Program and the Class of 1989 Study. *American Journal of Public Health, 82,* 1210-1216.

Perry, C. L., Klepp, K-I., Halper, A., Hawkins, H. G., & Murray, D. M. (1986). A process evaluation study of peer leaders in health education. *Journal of School Health, 56,* 62-67.

Perry, C. L., Klepp, K-I., & Sillers, C. (1989). Community-wide strategies for cardiovascular health: The Minnesota Heart Health Program Youth Program. *Health Education Research, 4,* 87-101.

Perry, C. L., Komro, K. A., Dudovitz, B., Veblen-Mortenson, S., Jeddeloh, R., Koele, R., Gallanar, I., Farbakhsh, K., & Stigler, M. H. (in press). An evaluation of a theater production to encourage non-smoking among elementary age children: 2 smart 2 smoke. *Tobacco Control.*

Perry, C. L., Luepker, R. V., Murray, D. M., Kurth, C., Mullis, R., Crockett, S., & Jacobs, D. J. (1988). Parent involvement with children's health promotion: The Minnesota Home Team. *American Journal of Public Health, 78,* 1156-1160.

Perry, C. L., Luepker, R. V., Murray, D. M., Hearn, M. D., Halper, A., Dudovitz, B., Maile, M. C., & Smyth, M. (1989). Parent involvement with children's health promotion: A one-year follow-up of the Minnesota Home Team. *Health Education Quarterly, 16,* 1156-1160.

Perry, C. L., Lytle, L. A., Feldman, H., Nicklas, T., Stone, E., Zive, M., Garceau, A., & Kelder, S. H. (1998). The effects of the Child and Adolescent Trial for Cardiovascular Health (CATCH) on fruit and vegetable consumption. *Journal of Nutrition Education, 30,* 354-360.

Perry, C. L., Maccoby, N., & McAlister, A. (1980). Adolescent smoking prevention; A third year follow-up. *World Smoking and Health, 5,* 40-45.

Perry, C. L., Mullis, R. M., & Maile, M. C. (1985). Modifying the eating behavior of young children. *Journal of School Health, 55,* 399-402.

Perry, C. L., Murray, D. M., & Griffin, G. (1990). Evaluating the statewide dissemination of smoking prevention curricula: Factors in teacher compliance. *Journal of School Health, 60,* 501-504.

Perry, C. L., Murray, D. M., & Klepp, K-I. (1987). Predictors of adolescent smoking and implications for prevention. *Morbidity and Mortality Weekly Report, 36,* 41-45.

Perry, C. L., Parcel, G. S., Stone, E. S., Nader, P. N., McKinlay, S. M., Luepker, R. V., & Webber, L. S. (1992). The Child and Adolescent Trial for Cardiovascular Health (CATCH): Overview of intervention program and evaluation methods. *Cardiovascular Risk Factors, 2,* 36-44.

Perry, C. L., Sellers, D., Johnson, C., Pedersen, S., Bachman, K., Parcel, G., Stone, E., Luepker, R. V., Wu, M., Nader, P., & Cook, K. W. (1997). The Child and Adolescent Trial for Cardiovascular Health (CATCH): Intervention, implementation, and feasibility for elementary schools in the U.S. *Health Education and Behavior, 24,* 716-735.

Perry, C. L., Stone, E. J., Parcel, G. S., Ellison, R. C., Nader, P., Webber, L. S., & Luepker, R. V. (1990). School based cardiovascular health promotion: The Child and Adolescent Trial for Cardiovascular Health (CATCH). *Journal of School Health, 60,* 406-413.

Perry, C. L., Williams, C. L., Forster, J. L., Wolfson, M., Wagenaar, A. C., Finnegan, J. R., McGovern, P. G., Veblen-Mortenson, S., Komro, K. A., & Anstine, P. S. (1993). Background, conceptualization, and design of a communitywide research program on adolescent alcohol use: Project Northland. *Health Education Research, 8,* 125-36.

Perry, C. L., Williams, C. L., Veblen-Mortenson, S., Toomey, T., Komro, K. A., Anstine, P. S., McGovern, P. G., Finnegan, J. R., Forster, J. L., Wagenaar, A. C., & Wolfson, M. (1996). Project Northland: Outcomes of a community-wide alcohol use prevention program during early adolescence. *American Journal of Public Health, 86,* 956-965.

Phillips, H. & Bradshaw, R. (1993). How customers actually shop: Customer interaction with the point of sale. *Journal of the Market Research Society, 35,* 51-62.

Pierce, J. P., Choi, W. S., Gilpin, E. A., Farkas, A. J., & Berry, C. C. (1998). Tobacco industry promotion of cigarettes and adolescent smoking. *Journal of the American Medical Association, 279,* 511-515.

Pierce, J. P., & Gilpin, F. A. (1995). A historical analysis of tobacco marketing and the uptake of smoking by youth in the United States: 1890-1977. *Health Psychology, 14,* 500-508.

Pierce, J. P., Lee, L., & Gilpin, F. A. (1994). Smoking initiation by adolescent girls; An association with targeted advertising. *Journal of the American Medical Association, 271,* 608-611.

Poland, B., Rootman, I., & Green, L. (Eds.). (in press). *Settings for health promotion.* Thousand Oaks, CA: Sage.

Pollay, R. L., Siddarth, S., Siegel, M., Haddix, A., Merritt, R. K., Giovino, G. A., & Eriksen, M. P. (1996). The last straw? Cigarette advertising and realized market shares among youths and adults. *Journal of Marketing, 60,* 1-16.

Prochaska, J. O., Redding, C. A., & Evers, K. E. (1997). The transtheoretical model and stages of change. In K. Glanz, F. M. Lewis, & B. K. Rimer (Eds.), *Health education and health behavior: Theory, research and practice* (pp. 60-84). San Francisco: Jossey-Bass.

Rappaport, J., Swift, C., & Hess, R. (Eds.). (1984). *Studies in empowerment: Steps toward understanding and action.* New York: Haworth.

Reinherz, H. Z., Giaconia, R. M., Silverman, A. B., Friedman, A., Pakiz, B., Frost, A. K., & Cohen, E. (1995). Early psychosocial risks for adolescent suicidal ideation and attempts. *Journal of the American Academy of Child and Adolescent Psychiatry, 34,* 599-611.

Resnick, M. D., Bearman, P. S., Blum, R. W., Bauman, K. E., Harris, K. M., Jones, J., Tabor, J., Beuhring, T., Sieving, R. E., Shew, M., Ireland, M., Bearinger, L. H., & Udry, J. R. (1997). Protecting adolescents from harm: Findings from the National Longitudinal Study on Adolescent Health. *Journal of the American Medical Association, 278,* 823-832.

Resnik, H. S., & Gibbs, J. (1981). Types of peer program approaches. *Adolescent peer pressure: Theory, correlates, and program implications for drug abuse prevention.* Rockville, MD: USDHHS.

Resnicow, K., & Allensworth, D. (1996). Conducting a comprehensive school health program. *Journal of School Health, 66,* 59-63.

Resnicow, K., Braithwaite, R. L., & Kuo, J. (1997). Interpersonal interventions for minority adolescents. In D. K. Wilson, J. R. Rodrigue, & W. C. Taylor (Eds.), *Health-promoting and health-compromising behaviors among minority adolescents.* Washington, DC: American Psychological Association.

Robinson, S. E., Morrow, S., Kigin, T., & Lindeman, M. (1991). Peer counselors in a high school setting: Evaluation of training and impact on students. *School Counselor, 39,* 35-40.

Roski, J., Perry, C. L., McGovern, P. G., Williams, C. L., Farbakhsh, K., & Veblen-Mortenson, S. (1997). School and community influences on adolescent alcohol and drug use. *Health Education Research, 12,* 255-266.

Saito, R. N., Benson, P. L., Blyth, D. A., & Sharma, A. R. (1995). *Places to grow: Perspectives on youth development opportunities for seven- to 14-year-old Minneapolis youth.* Minneapolis, MN: Search Institute.

Sallis, J. F. (1993). Promoting healthful diet and physical activity. In S. G. Millstein, A. C. Petersen, & E. O. Nightingale (Eds.), *Promoting the health of adolescents: New directions for the twenty-first century* (pp. 209-241). New York: Oxford University Press.

Schooler, C., Feighery, E., & Flora, J. A. (1996). Seventh graders' self-reported exposure to cigarette marketing and its relationship to their smoking behavior. *American Journal of Public Health, 86,* 1216-1221.

Sellers, D. E., McGraw, S. A., & McKinlay, J. B. (1994). Does the promotion and distribution of condoms increase teen sexual activity—Evidence from an HIV prevention program for Latino youth. *American Journal of Public Health, 84,* 1952-1959.

Silberman, M. (1998). *Active training* (2nd ed.). San Francisco: Jossey-Bass.

Simons-Morton, B., Parcel, G., & O'Hara, N. (1988). Promoting healthful diet and exercise behaviors in communities, schools, and families. *Family and Community Health, 11,* 25-35.

Smith, P. B., Weinman, M. L., & Parrilli, J. (1997). The role of condom motivation education in the reduction of new and reinfection rates of sexually transmitted diseases among inner-city female adolescents. *Patient Education & Counseling, 31,* 77-81.

Smyth, M. H. (1997). *Teacher characteristics and the sustainability of new health and nutrition curricula.* Unpublished master's thesis, Mankato State University, Mankato, MN.

Stone, E. J., Osganian, S. K., McKinlay, S. M., Wu, M. C., Webber, L. S., Luepker, R. V., Perry, C. L., Parcel, G. S., & Elder, J. P. (1996). Operational design and quality control in the CATCH multicenter trial. *Preventive Medicine, 25,* 384-399.

Strecher, V. J., & Rosenstock, I. M. (1997). The health belief model. In K. Glanz, F. M. Lewis, & B. K. Rimer (Eds.), *Health education and health behavior: Theory, research and practice* (pp. 41-59). San Francisco: Jossey-Bass.

Switzer, G. E., Simmons, R. G., Dew, M. A., Regalski, J. M., & Wang, C. H. (1995). The effect of a school-based helper program on adolescent self-image, attitudes, and behavior. *Journal of Early Adolescence, 15,* 429-454.

Telch, M., Killen, J., McAlister, A., Perry, C., & Maccoby. N. (1982). Long-term follow-up of a pilot project on smoking prevention with adolescents. *Journal of Behavioral Medicine, 5,* 1-8.

Tell, G. (1982). Factors influencing dietary habits: Experiences of the Oslo Youth Study. In T. J. Coates, A. C. Petersen, & C. L. Perry (Eds.), *Promoting adolescent health: A dialog on research and practice* (pp 381-396). Orlando, FL: Academic Press.

Trussell, J., Koenig, J., Steward, F., & Darroch, J. E. (1997). Medical care cost savings from adolescent contraceptive use. *Family Planning Perspectives, 29,* 248.

United States Department of Health and Human Services. (1994). *Preventing tobacco use among young people: A report of the Surgeon General.* Atlanta, GA: Author, CDC.

Veblen-Mortenson, S., Rissel, C. E., Perry, C. L., Forster, J., Wolfson, M., & Finnegan, J. R. (1999). Lessons learned from Project Northland: Community organization in rural communities. In N. Bracht (Ed.), *Health promotion at the community level* (2nd ed., pp. 105-117). Thousand Oaks, CA: Sage.

Wagenaar, A., & Perry, C. L. (1994). Community strategies for the reduction of youth drinking: Theory and application. *Journal of Research on Adolescence, 4,* 319-345.

Wallack, L., Dorfman, L., Jernigan, D., & Themba, M. (1993). *Media advocacy and public health: Power for prevention.* Thousand Oaks, CA: Sage.

Weissberg, R. P., Gullotta, T. P., Adams, G. R., Hampton, R. L., & Ryan, B. A. (Eds.). (1997). *Healthy children 2010: Enhancing children's wellness.* Thousand Oaks, CA: Sage.

Williams, C. L., Butcher, J. N., Ben-Porath, Y. S., & Graham, J. R. (1992). *MMPI-A content scales: Assessing psychopathology in adolescents.* Minneapolis: University of Minnesota Press.

Williams, C. L., & Perry, C. L. (1998). Design and implementation of parent programs for a community-wide adolescent alcohol use prevention program. *Journal of Prevention and Intervention in the Community, 17,* 65-80.

Williams, C. L., Perry, C. L., Dudovitz, B., Veblen-Mortenson, S., Anstine, P. S., Komro, K. A., & Toomey, T. (1995). A home-based prevention program for sixth grade alcohol use: Results from Project Northland. *Journal of Primary Prevention, 16,* 125-147.

Williams, C. L., Perry, C. L., Farbakhsh, K., & Veblen-Mortenson, S. (1999). Project Northland: Comprehensive alcohol use prevention for young adolescents, their parents, schools, peers, and communities. *Journal of Studies on Alcohol, Supp. No. 13,* 112-124.

Winkleby, M. A., Jatulis, D. E., Frank, E., & Fortmann, S. P. (1992). Socioeconomic status and health: How education, income, and occupation contribute to risk factors for cardiovascular disease. *American Journal of Public Health, 82,* 816-820.

Witkin, B. R., & Altschuld, J. W. (1995). *Planning and conducting needs assessments: A practical guide.* Thousand Oaks, CA: Sage.

World Cancer Research Fund. (1997). *Food, nutrition and the prevention of cancer: A global perspective.* Washington, DC: American Institute for Cancer Research.

World Health Organization. (1986). *Ottawa Charter for health promotion.* Geneva: Author.

AUTHOR INDEX

SUBJECT INDEX

ABOUT THE AUTHOR

Cheryl L. Perry, PhD, is Professor in the Division of Epidemiology, School of Public Health, at the University of Minnesota. She began her career as a junior high and high school teacher, and junior high school vice-principal, in Sacramento and Davis, California. She received her PhD from Stanford University and joined the faculty at the University of Minnesota in 1980. She has published more than 170 articles in the peer-reviewed literature on health promotion and prevention programs with children and adolescents. She was the senior scientific editor of the 1994 Surgeon General's Report on *Preventing Tobacco Use Among Young People* and currently serves as principal investigator of several community-wide health behavior research projects concerning eating patterns, tobacco and alcohol use, and violence among children and adolescents.